From our Kitchen to Yours

ALL-TIME-FAVORITE RECIPES

From

TENNESSEE
COOKS

Dedication

For every cook who wants to create amazing
recipes from the great state of Tennessee.

Appreciation

Thanks to all our Tennessee cooks who shared their
delightful and delicious recipes with us!

Gooseberry Patch
An imprint of Globe Pequot
246 Goose Lane
Guilford, CT 06437
www.gooseberrypatch.com
1 800 854 6673

Copyright 2021, Gooseberry Patch
978-162093-457-9

Do you have a tried & true recipe...tip, craft or
memory that you'd like to see featured in a
Gooseberry Patch cookbook? Visit our website at
www.gooseberrypatch.com and follow the easy steps
to submit your favorite family recipe.

Or send them to us at:

> Gooseberry Patch
> PO Box 812
> Columbus, OH 43216-0812

Don't forget to include the number of servings your
recipe makes, plus your name, address, phone
number and email address. If we select your recipe,
your name will appear right along with it...and you'll
receive a FREE copy of the book!

TENNESSEE COOKS

ICONIC TENNESSEE

From the low valleys to the coastal plains to the highest mountains, the Volunteer State's natural beauty is as broad as the Mississippi River that runs past it. Known for its deep-rooted musical history and the legendary Davy Crockett, Tennessee is brimming with a rich history that brings life to its culture and delicious recipes.

Tennessee's recipe heritage is a combination of Southeastern Indian, West European and West African cultural. Many cooks took spices, recipe ingredients and cooking traditions and then experimented to create delicious meals.

Tennesseeans are sure to gather at the table together for iconic foods like country ham, barbecue, cornbread, fried chicken and even a tall glass of Cheerwine soda or sweet tea.

The folks of Tennessee are not shy when it comes to how they prefer their food prepared...barbecued, fire roasted, pickled or chilled. Inside this book you'll see they all have a place at the Tennessee table!

You'll find everything from Honey-Mustard Spareribs, Fried Green Tomato Biscuits and Poor Man's Lobster to Old-Fashioned Banana Pudding, Tennessee Mud Cake in a Can and more! We know you will love this collection of tried & true recipes from cooks from all around the great state of Tennessee. Enjoy!

OUR STORY

Back in 1984, our families were neighbors in little Delaware, Ohio. With small children, we wanted to do what we loved and stay home with the kids too. We had always shared a love of home cooking and so, **Gooseberry Patch** was born.

Almost immediately, we found a connection with our customers and it wasn't long before these friends started sharing recipes. Since then we've enjoyed publishing hundreds of cookbooks with your tried & true recipes.

We know we couldn't have done it without our friends all across the country and we look forward to continuing to build a community with you. Welcome to the **Gooseberry Patch** family!

JoAnn & Vickie

TABLE OF CONTENTS

CHAPTER ONE

BEALE STREET BLUES

Breakfasts

ENJOY THESE TASTY BREAKFAST
RECIPES THAT BRING YOU TO THE
TABLE WITH A HEARTY "GOOD
MORNING!" AND CARRY YOU
THROUGH THE DAY TO TACKLE
WHATEVER COMES YOUR WAY.

BAKED PANCAKES WITH SAUSAGE

JILL VALENTINE
JACKSON, TN

My husband likes making breakfast for supper...I'll bake these while he scrambles the eggs!

1-3/4 c. all-purpose flour
4 t. baking powder
5 t. sugar
1 t. salt
3 eggs
1-1/2 c. milk
3 T. margarine, melted
1 lb. pork sausage
   breakfast links,
   browned and drained
Garnish: butter, warm
   syrup

Mix together flour, baking powder, sugar and salt; set aside. In a large bowl, beat eggs until fluffy; mix in milk and margarine. Gradually stir in flour mixture until smooth. Pour batter into a greased 15"x10" jelly-roll pan. Arrange sausages on top of batter. Bake at 450 degrees for 15 minutes, or until pancakes are done. Cut into squares and serve with butter and syrup.

Serves 8 to 10.

KITCHEN TIP

A crock of honey butter...so yummy on warm bread, biscuits and muffins. Simply blend together 1/2 cup each of honey and softened butter.

PB&J BREAKFAST BARS

**ANGIE FORESTER
MEMPHIS, TN**

This is our favorite quick breakfast item. My hubby can grab one of these as he walks out the door, because he always forgets to leave time for breakfast.

In a bowl, stir together oats, flour, brown sugar, baking soda, 1/4 teaspoon salt and cinnamon. Add melted butter and mix until crumbs form. Reserve 1/2 cup of oat mixture for topping; firmly spread remaining mixture in a lightly greased, parchment paper-lined 8"x8" baking pan. Bake at 350 degrees for 15 minutes, or until golden. In a bowl, beat together cream cheese, peanut butter, egg and remaining salt. Spread cream cheese mixture over baked crust; spread with jam. Top with reserved oat mixture. Bake for an additional 30 minutes, or until topping is golden; cool. Refrigerate for one hour, or until fully set. Cut into bars.

Makes 12 to 15.

1-1/2 c. quick-cooking oats, uncooked

1/2 c. all-purpose flour

1/2 c. light brown sugar, packed

1/4 t. baking soda

1/4 t. plus 1/8 t. salt, divided

1/4 t. cinnamon

6 T. butter, melted

8-oz. pkg. cream cheese, softened

1/2 c. creamy peanut butter

1 egg, beaten

1/2 c. favorite-flavor jam

AFTER–CHURCH EGG MUFFINS

MEGAN BROOKS
ANTIOCH, TN

I whip these up for my boys almost every Sunday after church...they start asking for them right when we walk in the door.

10-3/4 oz. can Cheddar cheese soup

1-1/2 c. milk

4 eggs

4 English muffins, split and toasted

3 T. butter, divided

4 slices Canadian bacon

In a bowl, mix together soup and milk. Fill 4 greased custard cups 1/4 full with soup mixture. Set cups on a baking sheet. Crack an egg into each cup, being careful not to break the yolks. Bake cups at 350 degrees for 12 minutes. Meanwhile, brown both sides of bacon in a skillet over medium heat. Top each muffin half with one teaspoon butter. Place 4 muffin halves on a baking sheet. Top each with a slice of bacon. Turn out a baked egg onto each bacon-topped muffin half. Drizzle remaining soup mixture over each egg. Top with other halves of muffins. Bake for an additional 2 minutes, or until heated through.

Makes 4 servings.

HEAT & HOLD SCRAMBLED EGGS

JUDY COLLINS
NASHVILLE, TN

Serve with a stack of buttered toast and a platter of sizzling sausage links...yum!

Combine all ingredients except butter in a large bowl. Whisk until smooth and set aside. Melt butter in a large skillet over low heat; pour egg mixture into skillet. Cook and stir until eggs are set to desired consistency. Can be held for up to one hour in a chafing dish or an electric skillet set at 200 degrees.

Serves 6.

1 doz. eggs, beaten
1-1/3 c. milk
1 t. salt
1/8 t. pepper
2 T. all-purpose flour
1 T. pimento, chopped
1 T. fresh parsley, chopped
1/4 c. butter

FRIED GREEN TOMATO BISCUITS

**CAROL HICKMAN
KINGSPORT, TN**

*These southern classics are great for a summertime breakfast or brunch!
Try one with a tall glass of sweet tea.*

16-oz. tube refrigerated
  buttermilk biscuits
1/2 lb. bacon
1 c. buttermilk
1-1/2 c. self-rising
  cornmeal
salt and pepper to taste
2 green tomatoes,
  thickly sliced
Garnish: mayonnaise

Bake biscuits according to package directions; set aside. In a large skillet, cook bacon until crisp; remove to paper towels to drain, reserving drippings in skillet. Pour buttermilk into a shallow bowl. On a small plate, combine cornmeal, salt and pepper. Dip tomato slices into buttermilk and then cornmeal mixture, until thickly coated on both sides. Fry tomatoes in reserved drippings over medium-high heat for 4 minutes per side, or until golden. Drain on paper towels. Split biscuits; spread one biscuit half with mayonnaise. Top with a tomato slice, bacon and top half of biscuit.

Serves 4 to 8.

JUST FOR FUN

Singers Aretha Franklin, Dolly Parton,
Kenny Chesney and Justin Timberlake,
were all born in Tennessee.

MAKE-AHEAD BRUNCH CASSEROLE

KELLY DALTON
LEWISBURG, TN

Assemble this casserole the night before...in the morning, just pop it in the oven. What a time-saver!

Melt butter in a skillet. Sauté onions and mushrooms until tender; set aside. Spread hashbrowns in a greased 13"x9" baking pan. Sprinkle with salt, pepper and garlic salt; top with bacon, onions and mushrooms. Whisk together eggs with milk and parsley; pour over casserole and top with cheese. Cover and refrigerate overnight. Bake, uncovered, at 400 degrees for one hour, or until set.

Makes 4 to 6 servings.

1 T. butter
2 onions, chopped
2 c. sliced mushrooms
4 c. frozen shredded
  hashbrowns, thawed
salt and pepper to taste
1/4 t. garlic salt
1 lb. bacon, crisply
  cooked and crumbled
4 eggs
1-1/2 c. milk
1/8 t. dried parsley
1 c. shredded Cheddar
  cheese

SKILLET STRAWBERRY JAM

MEGAN BROOKS
ANTIOCH, TN

This super-simple skillet jam is delectable spread on a freshly-baked homemade biscuit or a toasty English muffin.

4 c. strawberries, hulled and crushed
1/2 c. sugar
1 T. lemon juice
Optional: 1/4 t. vanilla extract

Combine strawberries, sugar and lemon juice in a skillet over medium-high heat; mix well. Cook, stirring often, until strawberries soften and mixture thickens, about 10 minutes. Remove from heat; stir in vanilla, if using. Store in an airtight jar in the refrigerator for up to 3 weeks.

Makes about 1-1/2 cups.

SAUSAGE GRAVY & BISCUITS

JILL VALENTINE
JACKSON, TN

My hubby loves this old-time diner favorite!

Brown sausage in a skillet over medium heat. Remove sausage to paper towels and set aside; wipe out skillet. Melt butter in same skillet; stir in flour and pepper. Slowly whisk in milk and soup. Bring to a boil; cook and stir until thick and bubbly. Stir in sausage; spoon mixture into a 4-quart slow cooker. Cover and cook on low setting for 6 to 8 hours. To serve, ladle gravy over warm split biscuits.

Serves 6.

1 lb. ground pork breakfast sausage
1/4 c. butter
1/4 c. all-purpose flour
pepper to taste
2 c. milk
10-3/4 oz. can Cheddar cheese soup
baked biscuits, split

HOT FRUIT BAKE

DONNA WILSON
MARYVILLE, TN

This is our family's Christmas breakfast tradition. It smells wonderful baking while we are opening our gifts.

- 21-oz. can cherry pie filling
- 20-oz. jar chunky applesauce
- 18-oz. can pineapple chunks, drained
- 15-oz. sliced peaches, drained
- 15-oz. can mandarin oranges, drained
- 1/2 c. brown sugar, packed
- 1 t. cinnamon
- 1/2 t. allspice

In a bowl, mix all ingredients together. Pour into an ungreased 2-quart casserole dish. Bake, uncovered, at 350 degrees for one hour, or until hot and bubbly.

Makes 8 servings.

COMPANY BREAKFAST CASSEROLE

JENA BUCKLER
BLOOMINGTON SPRINGS, TN

For a southwest flair, replace the mushrooms with a small can of sliced olives, add Monterey Jack cheese instead of Cheddar and serve with spicy salsa on the side.

Spread hashbrowns in a lightly greased 9"x9" baking pan. Layer ingredients as follows: half the onion, sausage, remaining onion, green pepper, mushrooms and cheese. In a separate bowl, mix eggs, milk and seasonings very well. Pour egg mixture over top of casserole; cover with aluminum foil and refrigerate overnight. In the morning, bake, covered, at 350 degrees for 45 to 60 minutes. Uncover and bake an additional 15 minutes, or until a knife inserted in center comes out clean.

Serves 8 to 10.

16-oz. pkg. shredded frozen hashbrowns, thawed
1 onion, chopped and divided
1 lb. ground pork sausage, browned and drained
1 green pepper, chopped
4-oz. can sliced mushrooms, drained
1/2 to 1 c. shredded Cheddar cheese
1 doz. eggs, beaten
1-1/2 c. milk
salt and pepper to taste
Optional: garlic salt to taste

CRUSTLESS HAM & SWISS PIE

SUSAN PAFFENROTH
JOHNSON CITY, TN

This pie couldn't be easier to stir up...it even makes its own crust.

2 c. cooked ham, shredded or diced

1 c. shredded Swiss cheese

1/3 c. onion, chopped

4 eggs, beaten

2 c. milk

1 c. biscuit baking mix

pepper, paprika and dried parsley to taste

Layer ham, cheese and onion in the bottom of a greased 10" deep-dish pie plate; set aside. Combine eggs, milk and baking mix in a blender; process for 15 seconds. Pour over ingredients in pie plate. Sprinkle with pepper, paprika and parsley to taste. Bake at 400 degrees for 30 to 40 minutes, or until golden and a knife tip comes out clean when inserted in center. Let stand for about 10 minutes to set; cut into wedges.

Serves 6.

PRESENTATION

If you're planning a family gathering, decorate your table to bring back childhood memories. Glue photocopies of old family photos to heavy paper for personalized table centerpieces.

JENN'S CRÈME BRÛLÉE FRENCH TOAST

JENNIFER DONNELLY
WOODLAWN, TN

I discovered a similar recipe in a cookbook and have since reworked it to satisfy my family's tastes. They love it!

In a small saucepan over medium heat, combine butter, brown sugar and corn syrup; cook and stir until smooth. Pour mixture into a 17"x12" greased jelly-roll pan. Spread to cover surface; sprinkle walnuts evenly over butter mixture. Arrange bread in a single layer to cover nuts and butter mixture. In a bowl, combine eggs, half-and-half, vanilla, cinnamon and salt. Using a ladle, spoon egg mixture over each bread slice. Sprinkle with more cinnamon, if desired. Cover and refrigerate overnight. Bake, uncovered, at 350 degrees for 30 minutes. Serve warm with syrup, if using. If not serving immediately, turn each slice of bread over once to prevent bread from sticking to the pan.

Serves 6 to 8.

1/2 c. butter
1 c. brown sugar, packed
2 T. corn syrup
1 c. chopped walnuts
12 slices Texas toast bread
5 eggs, beaten
1-1/2 c. half-and-half
1 t. vanilla extract
1 t. cinnamon
1/4 t. salt
Optional: additional cinnamon, maple syrup

LOADED BREAKFAST LOAF

JEANNETTE GROVES
OOLTEWAH, TN

My husband and I love to cook together! We're always creating new dishes. This one's a keeper.

8 eggs, beaten
3 c. self-rising flour
1 T. powdered sugar
1 T. baking powder
3/4 c. shortening
1-3/4 c. buttermilk
1 thick slice cooked ham, diced
4 slices cheese
1 egg, beaten

In a greased skillet over medium heat, stir eggs and cook until scrambled; set aside. In a bowl, combine flour, sugar, baking powder, shortening and buttermilk. On parchment paper, knead dough about a dozen times, or until no longer sticky; roll out to a 12-inch square, trimming edges if needed. Spread scrambled eggs, ham and cheese evenly over dough; roll up jelly-roll style. Fold in ends; lift parchment paper and transfer to a lightly greased 13"x9" baking pan. Brush loaf with beaten egg. Bake, uncovered, at 375 degrees for 20 to 25 minutes, until golden. Slice to serve.

Serves 6 to 8.

BACON BREAKFAST CASEROLE

ANDREA HICKERSON
TRENTON, TN

This is one of my most versatile recipes! It can be made up to a day ahead of time with just about any type of bread, breakfast meat and cheese you like. Simply refrigerate it until you're ready to bake.

Spray a 13"x9" baking pan with non-stick vegetable spray. Lay bread slices in the bottom of pan; spread bacon evenly over bread and set aside. In a large bowl, whisk together eggs, milk and seasonings; pour over bread. Spread cheese evenly over top. Bake, uncovered, at 350 degrees for 30 minutes, or until set. Cut into squares.

Serves 8 to 10.

6 slices white bread
1 lb. bacon, crisply cooked and crumbled
8 eggs, beaten
3 c. milk
1/4 t. salt
1/4 t. pepper
1/4 t. garlic powder
8-oz. pkg. shredded Cheddar cheese

FRUIT & NUT GRANOLA BARS

ELIZABETH MCCORD
MEMPHIS, TN

Granola bars are a favorite snack for kids and adults alike. These delicious bars are packed full of good stuff...so easy to make at home that you'll never buy them at the store again!

1-3/4 c. quick-cooking oats, uncooked

3/4 c. crispy rice cereal

1/2 c. brown sugar, packed

1/3 c. all-purpose flour

1/2 t. salt

1/2 t. cinnamon

1/2 c. shredded coconut

1 c. chopped walnuts

3/4 c. slivered almonds

3/4 c. raisins

5-oz. pkg. sweetened dried cherries

5-oz. pkg. sweetened dried cranberries

1/2 c. mini semi-sweet chocolate chips

2/3 c. canola oil

1/3 c. creamy peanut butter

1/3 c. honey

1/4 c. hot water

2 t. vanilla extract

In a large bowl, combine oats, cereal, brown sugar, flour, salt, cinnamon and coconut; toss well. Add nuts, dried fruits and chocolate chips. Toss again; set aside. In a small bowl, mix together remaining ingredients; spoon over oat mixture and mix well. Divide between 2 greased 11"x7" baking pans; press down to flatten. Bake, uncovered, at 350 degrees for 20 to 22 minutes, until edges are golden. Let cool in pans. Cut into bars and store in an airtight container.

Makes 16 bars.

SIMPLE SAUSAGE PIE

TASHA PETENZI
GOODLETTSVILLE, TN

This is a really easy breakfast dish that the whole family enjoys.
I like to make blueberry muffins to go along with it.

Spray a 9" pie plate with non-stick vegetable spray. Layer sausage and cheese in plate; set aside. In a bowl, whisk together eggs, milk and baking mix. Pour evenly over sausage and cheese. Bake, uncovered, at 400 degrees for 20 minutes, or until eggs are set and cheese is melted. Cut into wedges.

Serves 6.

1 lb. ground hot pork sausage, browned and drained
1-1/2 c. shredded Cheddar or casserole-blend cheese
2 eggs, beaten
1 c. milk
1/2 c. biscuit baking mix

FAMILY-TIME CONVERSATION

The "Grand Ole Opry" started as a country-music radio show in 1925. Today it's broadcast live from Nashville, where audiences can see stars like Carrie Underwood and groups such as Alabama Shakes perform.

BREAKFAST APPLE PIE

LORI HAINES
JOHNSON CITY, TN

This pie is actually easier to handle and serve after baking and cooling completely. I like to make it the day before, refrigerate it and warm it up in the microwave to serve. Be sure to serve it warm!

2/3 c. brown sugar, packed

2 T. cornstarch

1 t. cinnamon

1/2 t. nutmeg

1/4 t. ground cloves

2 lbs. Granny Smith apples, peeled, cored and diced

9-inch pie crust, unbaked

1/2 lb. bacon, cut into 1-inch pieces

1 c. shredded Cheddar cheese

In a large bowl, mix together brown sugar, cornstarch and spices. Add apples; toss to coat well. Spoon into unbaked pie crust. Separate uncooked bacon pieces and layer over apples. Cover loosely with aluminum foil. Bake at 350 degrees for one hour. Remove foil; continue baking for 15 minutes. If bacon is still not crisp enough, place pie under broiler, watching carefully. Allow pie to cool; rewarm before serving. Sprinkle cheese on top of warm pie. Cut into wedges.

Makes 6 to 8 servings.

SAVORY SAUSAGE SQUARES

**BOBBI GREENE
MOUNT JULIET, TN**

This dish is perfect for any get-together. It has only a few ingredients, it's easy to make and oh-so delicious! Be prepared to give out the recipe when you make it.

Combine sausage and water in a skillet over medium heat. Cook and crumble until sausage is no longer pink; drain and set aside. Unroll one tube of crescent roll dough and place into a greased 13"x9" baking pan. Top dough with sausage; sprinkle with cheese. Unroll remaining tube of dough and place over cheese. Brush the top with egg. Bake, uncovered, at 350 degrees for 20 to 25 minutes, until golden. Cut into squares to serve.

Serves 8 to 10.

- 1 lb. spicy ground pork breakfast sausage
- 1/2 c. water
- 2 8-oz. tubes refrigerated seamless crescent roll dough, divided
- 8-oz. pkg. shredded Cheddar cheese
- 1 egg, beaten

MINI EGG, TOMATO & SPINACH BREAKFAST PIZZAS

MEGAN BROOKS
ANTIOCH, TN

*My teenagers are old enough to make these mini pizzas themselves.
When they have friends to stay overnight, they'll raid the fridge to find other
yummy toppings to add.*

6 eggs

2 T. shredded Parmesan cheese

4 6-inch mini flatbreads

Optional: 2 t. olive oil

1 c. cherry tomatoes, halved

1/2 c. fresh spinach, thinly sliced

salt and pepper to taste

3/4 c. shredded pizza-blend cheese

Optional: red pepper flakes to taste

Whisk together eggs and Parmesan cheese in a bowl. Pour mixture into a greased large skillet over medium heat. Cook, stirring occasionally, until eggs are lightly scrambled. Do not overcook. Place flatbreads on a baking sheet; lightly brush tops with oil, if desired. Divide scrambled eggs, tomatoes and spinach evenly among flatbreads. Season with salt and pepper; top with shredded cheese. Bake at 450 degrees for 5 to 6 minutes, until cheese is melted. Sprinkle with red pepper flakes, if desired. Cut into wedges; serve immediately.

Serves 4.

JUST FOR FUN

The Great Smoky Mountains are known as the "Salamander Capital of the World," and the park alone has 30 different species.

COUNTRY HASHBROWN CASSEROLE

BECCA JONES
JACKSON, TN

Several years ago I was thumbing through my cookbooks and found this recipe. It has definitely been a keeper. I hope your family enjoys it as much as mine does!

Combine potatoes, cheese and onion in a greased 3-quart casserole dish; set aside. Combine remaining ingredients in a bowl; pour over potato mixture and stir well. Bake, uncovered, at 425 degrees for 45 to 60 minutes, until bubbly and golden.

Serves 10.

26-oz. pkg. frozen country-style hashbrown potatoes
2 c. Colby or mild Cheddar cheese, shredded
1/4 c. onion, minced
1 c. milk
1/2 c. chicken broth
2 T. butter, melted
1/8 t. garlic powder
1 t. salt
1/4 t. pepper

KITCHEN TIP

For hosting a stress-free brunch, focus on make-ahead meals like baked French toast and egg casseroles. Save recipes that need to be cooked on the spot, like pancakes and omelets for smaller family breakfasts.

CAMPFIRE JELLY BISCUITS

LAUREN GEDDINGS
KNOXVILLE, TN

We spent many summer holidays tent camping in the Great Smoky Mountains. Part of our breakfast tradition always included my mother's famous campfire jelly biscuits. The biscuits are made from scratch and baked over the coals of the campfire. We would roll them out on floured wax paper covering the picnic table.

5 c. all-purpose flour
1 T. baking powder
1 t. baking soda
2 t. salt
1 c. shortening
1 env. active dry yeast
1/4 c. warm water
1-1/2 c. buttermilk
1/2 c. butter
1/2 c. strawberry
  preserves

While campfire coals are still glowing, lay a large rack across coals. Whisk together flour, baking powder, baking soda and salt. Cut in shortening. Dissolve yeast in warm water, about 110 to 115 degrees. Stir in buttermilk; add to dry ingredients. Stir well and knead, adding more flour if necessary. Roll out on floured wax paper to about one-inch thick. With a 3-inch round cookie cutter, cut out 10 biscuits. Spray a 9" round cake pan with non-stick vegetable spray. Place biscuits in pan; cover tightly with aluminum foil. Place pan on rack over coals. Check for doneness after 20 minutes. Split biscuits; place a dollop of butter and preserves on each. Replace biscuit tops and wrap each biscuit in aluminum foil. Return to rack for 5 minutes, until butter melts and preserves are warm.

Makes 10.

SPEEDY SAUSAGE MUFFINS

LISA GIBBS
NASHVILLE, TN

My mother-in-law bakes these muffins for us. She serves them with hot coffee and spiced tea...so nice on a cool morning!

Combine sausage, baking mix and cheese in a large bowl; make a well in the center of mixture. Stir together soup and water; add to sausage mixture, stirring just until combined. Spoon into lightly greased muffin cups, filling to top of cups. Bake at 375 degrees for 20 to 25 minutes, until lightly golden. Serve warm.

Makes 16 muffins.

1 lb. ground pork sausage, browned and drained

3 c. biscuit baking mix

1-1/2 c. shredded Cheddar cheese

10-3/4 oz. can Cheddar cheese soup

3/4 c. water

COTTAGE CHEESE SCRAMBLED EGGS

JILL VALENTINE
JACKSON, TN

Whenever I spent the night at her house in the country, Granny used to fix this for me with eggs from her own chickens. Delicious!

6 eggs
3/4 c. small-curd
   cottage cheese
2 T. milk
1 T. fresh chives,
   chopped
1/2 t. salt
1/8 t. pepper
2 T. butter

In a bowl, beat eggs lightly. Stir in cottage cheese, milk, chives, salt and pepper. Melt butter in a skillet over low heat; add egg mixture. Turn egg mixture with a spatula as it begins to thicken; do not stir. Cook just until set; serve immediately.

Serves 4.

APPLE GEM CAKES

LORRIE SMITH
DRUMMONDS, TN

*This tasty recipe for fruit muffins came from my Grandmother Agnes.
She always called muffins by the old-fashioned name of "gem cakes."*

Sift flour and sugar together into a bowl. Add apple;
mix well. In a separate bowl, combine egg, milk and
butter. Add to flour mixture and stir just enough to
moisten. Spoon into muffin cups that have been
sprayed with non-stick vegetable spray, filling 3/4 full.
Combine remaining ingredients; sprinkle over batter.
Bake at 400 degrees for 15 to 20 minutes.

Makes one dozen.

2 c. self-rising flour

1/2 c. sugar

1 c. apple, cored, peeled
and finely chopped

1 egg, beaten

1 c. milk

3 T. butter, melted and
slightly cooled

1/3 c. brown sugar,
packed

1/2 c. chopped pecans or
walnuts

1/2 t. cinnamon

HOMEMADE DOUGHNUTS

MEGAN BROOKS
ANTIOCH, TN

Doughnuts are a BIG Halloween tradition at Grandma's house. My grandmother is eighty-five and she still makes these doughnuts for all her grandchildren and great-grandchildren when they come to her house trick-or-treating. Frightfully delicious!

2 c. biscuit baking mix
1 c. sugar, divided
1/3 c. milk
1 egg, beaten
1 t. vanilla extract
oil for deep frying
1/4 t. cinnamon
1/4 t. nutmeg

Mix together baking mix, 1/4 cup sugar, milk, egg and vanilla until well blended. Turn dough onto a lightly floured surface; knead about 10 times. Roll out to 3/8-inch thick. Cut with a floured doughnut cutter. Add oil to 3 inches depth in a heavy skillet or deep-fat fryer. Heat oil to 375 degrees over medium-high heat. Drop doughnuts into hot oil, a few at a time. Fry until golden on both sides, about one minute per side. Remove doughnuts with a slotted spoon; drain on paper towels. Combine remaining sugar and spices in a small paper bag. Add doughnuts to bag, a few at a time, and shake to coat. Serve warm.

Makes about 1-1/2 dozen.

CUSTARDY FRENCH TOAST

SARAH CAMERON
MARYVILLE, TN

Absolutely the best French toast you'll ever eat!

In a large shallow bowl, whisk eggs, cream, milk, sugar and cinnamon until well blended. Dip bread slices one at a time into egg mixture, turning to allow both sides to absorb mixture. Melt one tablespoon butter on a non-stick griddle over medium heat. Cook for about 4 minutes per side, until golden and firm to the touch. Repeat with remaining butter and bread. Dust with powdered sugar, if desired. Serve with warm cinnamon syrup.

Cinnamon Syrup:

Combine water and brown sugar in a heavy saucepan. Bring to a boil over high heat, stirring until sugar dissolves. Boil until syrup reduces to one cup, about 10 minutes. Remove from heat; whisk in cream and cinnamon. Serve warm. Syrup may be refrigerated, then rewarmed at serving time.

Serves 6 to 8.

6 eggs, beaten
3/4 c. whipping cream
3/4 c. milk
1/4 c. sugar
1/4 t. cinnamon
1 loaf French bread, thickly sliced
2 T. butter, divided
Optional: powdered sugar
Garnish: cinnamon syrup

CINNAMON SYRUP
1 c. water
2 T. whipping cream
1 c. dark brown sugar, packed
1/2 t. cinnamon

CINNAMON ROLLS

PEGGY PELFREY
ASHLAND CITY, TN

This recipe is easy to make for a leisurely brunch or a sleep-in Saturday or Sunday morning. The house fills with the delicious smell of cinnamon rolls...yummy!

1/4 c. butter, melted
1 t. vanilla extract
1/2 c. brown sugar, packed
1 T. plus 1 t. cinnamon, divided
12-oz. can refrigerated biscuits
Optional: chopped pecans
1-1/3 c. powdered sugar
2 T. milk

In a small bowl, mix together melted butter and vanilla; set aside. In a separate bowl, combine brown sugar and one teaspoon cinnamon. Roll biscuits in butter mixture, then in brown sugar mixture until well coated. Place biscuits in a slow cooker lightly sprayed with non-stick cooking spray; sprinkle with pecans, if using. Place a paper towel on top of slow cooker and cover with lid. Cover and cook on low setting for 2 to 3 hours. Meanwhile, mix together powdered sugar, milk and remaining cinnamon in a small bowl. When rolls are done, drizzle with glaze.

Serves 8.

RING
L
COOKEVILLE
MARYVILLE
JULIET
OAK RIDGE
MORRISTOWN - BRISTOL -

QUINOA BREAKFAST BAKE

LORI HAINES
JOHNSON CITY, TN

It's terrific to have this casserole tucked in the freezer to serve at a moment's notice! The original recipe came from a B & B. I've changed some of the ingredients to fit my family's taste.

Mix all ingredients in a bowl. Spoon into an 11"x9" baking pan sprayed with non-stick vegetable spray. Bake, uncovered, at 350 degrees for one hour. Let cool slightly; cut into squares and serve warm. To freeze, wrap squares in plastic wrap; store in a plastic freezer bag in the freezer. To reheat, microwave individual squares for 2 minutes.

Makes 18 to 24 servings.

2 lbs. ground pork breakfast sausage, browned and drained

16-oz. pkg. shredded Colby Jack cheese

3 c. cooked quinoa

1 c. milk

4 eggs, beaten

1 T. dried oregano

1 t. garlic, minced

CHAPTER TWO

SOUTHERN-STYLE

Salads, Sides & Breads

TOSS TOGETHER GREAT TASTE AND HEALTHY GOODNESS TO MAKE FRESH, SATISFYING AND TASTY SALADS THAT ARE PACKED WITH FULL-ON FLAVOR.

THUMBS-UP CORNBREAD SALAD

JANA TIMMONS
HENDERSONVILLE, TN

Be sure to get your share early...it'll be gone before you know it!

8-1/2 oz. pkg. cornbread mix

24-oz. can pinto beans, drained and rinsed

2 15-oz. cans corn, drained

1/4 c. sweet onion, diced

1 c. cherry tomatoes, quartered

1/3 c. celery, chopped

1/2 c. bacon bits, divided

2 c. shredded 4-cheese blend cheese, divided

1 c. sour cream

2 c. ranch salad dressing

Prepare and bake cornbread according to package directions; set aside to cool. Crumble cornbread into a large serving bowl. Add beans, corn, onion, tomatoes, celery, 1/4 cup bacon bits and 1-1/2 cups cheese. Toss well; set aside. In another bowl, mix sour cream and salad dressing together; drizzle over cornbread mixture and toss to coat. Sprinkle with remaining bacon bits and cheese.

Serves 10.

KING
L
COOKEVILLE
MARYVILLE
JULIET
OAK RIDGE
MORRISTOWN - BRISTOL

BLACK-EYED PEA SALAD

ANNETTE SYKES
SPRINGFIELD, TN

My friends & family always ask me to bring this unique salad to potluck suppers.

Combine onion, parsley, vinegar, oil, garlic and salt in a large bowl. Add peas and tomato; chill. At serving time, arrange lettuce on a platter. Spoon mixture over lettuce. Garnish with tomato wedges and green pepper rings.

Serves 6 to 8.

1/3 c. onion, grated

1/3 c. fresh parsley, minced

3 T. cider vinegar

2 T. oil

1 clove garlic, minced

1/4 t. salt

2 16-oz. cans black-eyed peas, drained

1 tomato, diced

1 head lettuce, shredded

Garnish: tomato wedges, green pepper rings

GREEN BEAN BUNDLES

WENDY SENSING
BRENTWOOD, TN

Easy and delicious! This is one of our favorite side dishes to bring to church get-togethers...the dish always comes home empty.

3 14-1/2 oz. cans whole green beans, drained

8 slices bacon, cut in half crosswise

6 T. butter, melted

1/2 c. brown sugar, packed

2 to 3 cloves garlic, minced

Gather beans in bundles of 10; wrap each bundle with a half-slice of bacon. Arrange bundles, seam-side down, in a lightly greased 13"x9" baking pan. Mix melted butter, brown sugar and garlic in a small bowl; spoon over bundles. Cover and bake at 375 degrees for 30 minutes. Uncover; bake an additional 15 minutes.

Serves 6.

FRESH TOMATO PIE

**LYNETTE EDMONDSON
DICKSON, TN**

A delightful way to prepare sun-ripe tomatoes fresh from the farmstand!

Place tomatoes between paper towels to absorb some of the moisture. Remove tomatoes to a bowl and sprinkle with salt and pepper. In a separate bowl, combine mayonnaise, cheeses, chives and basil; carefully add tomatoes. Pour mixture into pie crust. Bake at 400 degrees for 20 to 30 minutes.

Makes 8 servings.

3 to 4 tomatoes, diced
salt and pepper to taste
1/2 c. mayonnaise
1 c. shredded sharp Cheddar cheese
1 c. shredded Colby Jack cheese
1 T. dried chives
1 T. dried basil
9-inch pie crust, baked

PRESENTATION

Simple garnishes dress up main dishes all year 'round! Fresh mint sprigs add coolness and color to summertime dishes, while rosemary sprigs and cranberries add a festive touch to holiday platters.

FRIED TATERS & SQUASH

LAUREN AYERS
ATOKA, TN

My father-in-law taught me how to make this simple dish. It was his mother's recipe. Take one bite and you'll want more...that's how good it is!

canola oil for frying
5 to 6 redskin potatoes, peeled and cubed
3/4 c. onion, chopped
3 summer squash, thinly sliced into rounds
salt and pepper to taste

Add one inch canola oil to a large skillet. Heat over medium heat until hot but not smoking. Add vegetables; season with salt and pepper. Cover and cook about 20 minutes, until tender and golden. Drain on paper towels before serving.

Makes 4 servings.

COUNTRY CORNBREAD

GLENDA BOLTON
DANDRIDGE, TN

My mother made this cornbread for as long as I can remember. She cooked it in a pan on top of the stove. My only change is that I bake mine in a cast-iron skillet in the oven.

5 T. oil, divided
2 c. self-rising cornmeal
3/4 c. self-rising flour
2 c. buttermilk
2 eggs, beaten

Brush a 9" to 10" cast-iron skillet generously with one tablespoon oil. Set oven to 450 degrees; place skillet on a rack in center of oven. Meanwhile, in a large bowl, stir together cornmeal and flour; make a well in the center. In a separate bowl, whisk together buttermilk, eggs and remaining oil. Pour buttermilk mixture into the well in cornmeal mixture; stir just until moistened. Carefully remove hot skillet from oven; pour in batter. Bake at 450 degrees for 15 to 20 minutes, until cornbread springs back when pressed in the center. Let stand for 5 minutes; turn cornbread out onto a plate or serve directly from the skillet.

Makes 8 servings.

SEASONED GREENS & BACON

GLENDA BOLTON
DANDRIDGE, TN

An original recipe that I developed. My family always added vinegar after the greens were cooked. I wanted to find out how they would taste if vinegar & other items were added while the greens cooked...they're delicious!

In a heavy stockpot over medium-high heat, bring water to a boil. Add remaining ingredients; reduce heat to medium-low. Simmer until greens are tender, one to 2 hours, stirring occasionally.

Makes 6 to 8 servings.

4 c. water

4 to 5 cubes chicken bouillon

1 to 2 lbs. turnip and/ or mustard greens, chopped

1/2 lb. bacon or hog jowl, cut into 1-inch pieces

3/4 c. onion, very finely chopped

1 T. garlic, minced

1/4 c. vinegar, or to taste

salt and pepper to taste

Optional: 1/8 t. cayenne pepper

CLOVERLEAF TATER ROLLS

LINDA RICH
BEAN STATION, TN

My mother and her sisters all made yeast rolls often. This recipe was their favorite. Every time we had a family gathering, you could count on these rolls being there. They take some time to make, but are worth the effort. The leftover rolls are great if reheated.

1 c. mashed potatoes
2/3 c. shortening
1/3 c. sugar
1-1/2 t. salt
2 eggs, beaten
1 env. active dry yeast
1/2 c. warm water, 110 to 115 degrees
1 c. warm milk, 110 to 115 degrees
6 to 8 c. all-purpose flour
1/2 c. butter, melted

Warm potatoes in a microwave-safe dish; add potatoes to a large bowl. Add shortening, sugar, salt and eggs; mix well and set aside. In a cup, dissolve yeast in warm water; add warm milk. Add yeast mixture to potato mixture; mix well and stir in enough flour to make a stiff dough. Knead dough well on a floured surface. Place dough in a greased large bowl; cover with a tea towel and let rise in a warm place until double in bulk, about 2 to 3 hours. Knead dough slightly; brush top with melted butter. At this point, dough may be covered and refrigerated, then baked later. Shape dough into 36 small balls. Place 3 balls in each of 12 greased muffin cups. Cover and let rise until double in bulk, about 2 to 3 hours. Bake at 400 degrees for 15 to 20 minutes, until golden.

Makes one dozen.

SHOEPEG CORN SALAD

RENEE WHITED
MONTEREY, TN

This is one of my favorite recipes to take to potlucks and family reunions. It's so tasty that it's hard to believe how simple it is to make! Every time I take this dish, someone requests the recipe.

In a large serving bowl, combine corn, cucumber, onion and tomatoes. Stir in mayonnaise or salad dressing. Season with salt and pepper to taste. Cover and chill.

Makes 8 servings.

- 2 15-oz. cans white shoepeg corn, drained
- 1 cucumber, diced
- 1/2 c. red onion, or 3 to 4 green onions, diced
- 1 to 2 tomatoes, diced
- 1/4 c. mayonnaise or mayonnaise-style salad dressing
- salt and pepper to taste

PARMESAN-TOMATO ORZO

AMY BELL
ARLINGTON, TN

We enjoy this tasty, simple side with Chicken Parmesan instead of spaghetti. Serve with additional sauce, if you wish.

Melt butter in a heavy skillet over medium-high heat. Stir orzo into skillet; sauté until lightly golden. Stir in broth and bring to a boil. Cover; reduce heat and simmer until orzo is tender and liquid is absorbed, about 15 to 20 minutes. Mix in cheese and sauce; serve warm.

Serves 4.

- 2 T. butter
- 1 c. orzo pasta, uncooked
- 2-1/2 c. chicken broth
- 1/2 c. grated Parmesan cheese
- 2 T. Italian-seasoned tomato sauce

DILLED NEW POTATO SALAD

LINDA STONE
COOKEVILLE, TN

No summer buffet table is complete without a big bowl of potato salad. This recipe is extra scrumptious with the fresh flavors of new potatoes, sweet onion and dill. You and your guests will love it!

2 lbs. new potatoes, cut into wedges
10-oz. pkg. frozen petite sweet peas, thawed and drained
1/2 c. mayonnaise
1/2 c. plain yogurt
1 sweet onion, chopped
3 T. fresh dill, minced
1 T. Dijon mustard
1 t. garlic salt
1/4 t. pepper

In a saucepan over medium-high heat, cover potatoes with water. Cook for 20 minutes, or until tender. Drain and add peas. In a large bowl, stir together remaining ingredients. Add potato mixture; toss gently to coat. Cover and chill at least 2 hours.

Serves 8.

EASY BUTTERMILK ROLLS

LINDA RICH
BEAN STATION, TN

My mother made these cloverleaf rolls often...they are easy and quick for yeast rolls. Only 90 minutes to make.

2-3/4 c. all-purpose flour
2 T. sugar
1/2 t. baking soda
1/2 t. salt
1 env. quick-rise dry yeast
1 c. buttermilk, heated to lukewarm
1/4 c. shortening
Garnish: melted butter

Combine flour, sugar, baking soda and salt; set aside. Add yeast to buttermilk; stir in shortening. Add buttermilk mixture to flour mixture; stir well. Let rise 45 minutes, or until double in bulk. Work down dough and shape into small balls. Place in a greased muffin tin, adding 3 balls to each cup. Brush tops with melted butter. Let rise again until double, about 30 minutes; Bake at 375 degrees for 20 to 30 minutes, until golden.

Makes one dozen.

SAVORY SOUTHERN CASSEROLE

PAULA EGGLESTON
KNOXVILLE, TN

In the South, grits are eaten with any meal of the day. This cheesy dish is great for a family cookout or barbecue.

Bring water, onion and salt to a boil; add grits. Remove from heat; stir to keep smooth. In a separate saucepan, melt 1/2 cup butter, cheese and garlic powder. In a small bowl, beat eggs with enough milk to make one cup; add to cheese mixture. Stir cheese mixture into grit mixture; pour into a greased 13"x9" baking pan. Melt remaining butter; stir in cereal. Sprinkle on top of grits. Bake at 350 degrees for 30 minutes.

Serves 8 to 10.

4 c. water

1 onion, chopped

1 t. salt

1 c. quick-cooking grits, uncooked

3/4 c. butter, divided

1-1/2 lbs. pasteurized process cheese spread, cubed

garlic powder to taste

4 eggs

milk

2 c. corn flake cereal

LIGHT APPLE WALDORF SALAD

JANET SHARP
MILFORD, OH

If you like Waldorf salad, you will enjoy this healthy lighter version. It is especially delicious with pork tenderloin.

10-oz. pkg. romaine lettuce or fresh spinach, torn

2 apples, cored and sliced

1 c. seedless grapes, halved

1 c. celery, sliced

1 c. walnut halves, toasted

RED WINE VINEGAR DRESSING

1/2 c. olive oil

1/4 c. red wine vinegar

salt and pepper to taste

Combine all salad ingredients in bowl. Just before serving, pour desired amount of Red Wine Vinegar Dressing over salad. Toss well and serve immediately.

Red Wine Vinegar Dressing:

Shake ingredients well in a covered jar or process well in a blender. Keep refrigerated.

Makes 4 servings.

GREAT-AUNT'S BROCCOLI-CAULIFLOWER SALAD

RENEE JOHNSON
COOKEVILLE, TN

This recipe was given to me by my Great-Aunt Elizabeth. She was my grandmother's sister, and they were both wonderful cooks. This is a good dish to take to potlucks.

Combine salad dressing, sour cream, sugar and vinegar; stir well. Cover and chill for 6 hours. At serving time, combine vegetables in a large bowl. Pour dressing mixture over vegetables and mix well.

Makes 8 servings.

1 c. mayonnaise-type salad dressing
1/2 c. sour cream
1 T. sugar
1 T. vinegar
5 c. broccoli flowerets
2-1/2 c. cauliflower flowerets
1 c. onion, chopped
2 c. cherry tomatoes

KITCHEN TIP

A melon baller has lots of uses besides making juicy fruit salads. Put it to work forming perfect balls of cookie dough, coring apples and even making pretty little servings of butter for the dinner table. Clever!

ALL-TIME-FAVORITE RECIPES FROM TENNESSEE COOKS

MISS SHERYL'S CORNBREAD MUFFINS

**KRISTINA SOLID
FAYETTEVILLE, TN**

Cornbread muffins aren't hard to make from scratch. This tasty recipe was given to me by a dear friend. My children ask for them for dinner all the time!

1 c. cornmeal
1 c. all-purpose flour
1/2 c. sugar
2-1/2 t. baking powder
1/4 t. salt
1 c. buttermilk
1/2 c. butter, softened
1 egg, beaten

Mix cornmeal, flour, sugar, baking powder and salt in a large bowl; set aside. Combine remaining ingredients in a separate bowl; add to cornmeal mixture. Stir until moistened. Divide batter evenly into 12 lightly greased muffin cups. Bake at 400 degrees for 15 to 20 minutes.

Makes one dozen.

ANGEL BISCUITS

LORRIE OWENS
MUNFORD, TN

This is my grandmother's recipe. Just smelling these heavenly biscuits while they bake brings back wonderful memories.

In a cup, stir yeast into water until dissolved; set aside. In a large bowl, combine flour, sugar, baking powder, baking soda and salt; mix well. Add yeast mixture, shortening and buttermilk; stir well. Turn dough onto a floured surface and knead lightly. Roll out dough about 1/2-inch thick. Cut out with a 2" biscuit cutter. Place biscuits on an ungreased baking sheet; brush with melted butter. Bake at 400 degrees for 12 to 15 minutes, until lightly golden.

Makes about 2-1/2 dozen.

1 env. active dry yeast
2 T. warm water, 110 to 115 degrees
5 c. all-purpose flour
3 T. sugar
3 T. baking powder
1 t. baking soda
1 t. salt
1 c. shortening
2 c. buttermilk

Garnish: melted butter

JUST FOR FUN

Graceland, singer Elvis Presley's Memphis mansion, gets more visitors than any other U.S. home except for the White House.

SUMMERTIME PASTA SALAD

CRYSTAL KIRBY
MURFREESBORO, TN

This recipe is great for church picnics and potlucks. Not only is it easy to prepare, but it can be tossed together the day before. Everyone comes back for more...even the kiddies like it!

13-1/4 oz. pkg. whole-wheat elbow macaroni, cooked, drained and cooled

1/2 c. green pepper, chopped

1/2 c. red pepper, chopped

10-oz. container grape tomatoes

3-1/2 oz. pkg. pepperoni, quartered

1/2 c. red onion, chopped

8-oz. pkg. Cheddar cheese cubes

16-oz. bottle Italian salad dressing

Mix all ingredients except salad dressing together in a large bowl with a lid. Add salad dressing to taste; toss to mix well. Refrigerate for at least 4 hours up to 24 hours, stirring or shaking occasionally. Keep refrigerated until ready to serve.

Makes 10 to 15 servings.

MAMA'S CUCUMBER SALAD

VIRGINIA SHAW
MEDON, TN

I used to take this salad to my sons' baseball award dinners and picnics. Children and adults alike always request this salad...it's cool, refreshing and very simple to make.

Toss together vegetables in a large bowl; pour salad dressing over all and toss to mix. Cover and refrigerate at least 3 hours to overnight.

Makes 8 to 10 servings.

2 cucumbers, sliced

1 bunch green onions, diced or 1 red onion, sliced and separated into rings

2 to 3 tomatoes, diced

16-oz. bottle zesty Italian salad dressing

HOT DEVILED OKRA

LINDA BARKER
MOUNT PLEASANT, TN

My grandmother used to make this recipe years ago and it was passed on to me. She raised the vegetables in her garden.

Mix cornmeal and pepper in a shallow dish. Dip okra, tomatoes and jalapeño into mixture, coating well. Heat drippings or oil in a skillet over medium-high heat. Add vegetables to skillet and cook for several minutes, until golden. Drain on paper towels.

Makes 6 to 8 servings.

1 c. self-rising cornmeal

pepper to taste

1 lb. okra, cut into 1/4-inch rings

2 green tomatoes, chopped

1 jalapeño pepper, seeded and chopped

1/3 c. bacon drippings or oil for frying

AUNT PUP'S QUICK ROLLS

BECCA BRASFIELD
BURNS, TN

*My Aunt Pup was famous in our family for not being the greatest
cook, but everyone loved her quick & easy rolls. They are simple to
make and taste great! The rolls may be made ahead and stored in
the refrigerator; just bake them a little longer.*

1/2 c. butter, melted

Optional: 1 T. dried,
minced onion, 1 T.
dried parsley, 1 T.
dried chives, 1/4 t.
garlic powder

2 c. biscuit baking mix

8-oz. container sour
cream onion,

Place butter in a large bowl; stir in desired
seasonings. Add biscuit mix and sour cream; stir just
until moistened. Spoon batter into greased muffin
cups. Bake at 400 degrees for 15 to 20 minutes, until
lightly golden. Serve immediately. May be baked
alongside a casserole at 350 degrees for 30 to 35
minutes.

Makes one dozen.

RING
L
COOKEVILLE
MARYVILLE
JULIET
OAK RIDGE
MORRISTOWN — BRISTOL

COUNTRY CORN PUDDING

ANGELA LIVELY,
BAXTER, TN

With four kinds of corn, this new twist on an old favorite is scrumptious!

In a large bowl, mix all ingredients well; pour into a slow cooker. Cover and cook on low setting for 5 to 6 hours, stirring after 3 hours. Garnish with fresh parsley.

Serves 8.

16-oz. pkg. frozen corn

2 11-oz. cans sweet corn & diced peppers

14-3/4 oz. can creamed corn

6-1/2 oz. pkg. corn muffin mix

3/4 c. water

1/4 c. butter, melted

1 t. salt

Garnish: fresh parsley, chopped

CINNAMON APPLESAUCE MUFFINS

**AMANDA HENSLEY
CHURCH HILL, TN**

Equally yummy at breakfast or with a warming bowl of soup.

1/2 c. butter, softened
3/4 c. sugar
2 eggs, beaten
1 t. vanilla extract
1-3/4 c. all-purpose flour
1 t. baking powder
1 t. baking soda
1 T. cinnamon
1/8 t. salt
1/4 c. sour cream
1 c. applesauce

In a large bowl, beat butter and sugar with an electric mixer on medium speed. Beat in eggs and vanilla; set aside. In a separate bowl, mix flour, baking powder, baking soda, cinnamon and salt. Add flour mixture, sour cream and applesauce to butter mixture. Stir batter by hand until blended. Fill greased muffin cups 2/3 full. Bake at 375 degrees for 15 to 20 minutes.

Makes one dozen.

PECAN PIE MUFFINS

SANDY GLENNEN
DANDRIDGE, TN

Perfectly nutty and sweet! Oh-so-good with a cup of tea.

In a bowl, stir together all ingredients except pecan halves. Fill greased mini muffin cups 2/3 full. Top each with a pecan half, if using. Bake at 350 degrees for 12 to 15 minutes, until golden.

Makes 2-1/2 to 3 dozen.

1 c. light brown sugar, packed
1/2 c. all-purpose flour
2 eggs, beaten
2/3 c. butter, melted
1 c. chopped pecans
Optional: pecan halves

FABULOUS BAKED POTATO CASSEROLE

GINIA JOHNSTON
GREENEVILLE, TN

Make sure to get some quick, because this delectable dish always disappears first at every gathering!

6 to 7 potatoes, peeled and cubed

2 c. shredded Cheddar cheese

1 c. mayonnaise

1/2 c. sour cream

1 onion, diced

6 slices bacon, crisply cooked and crumbled

In a large saucepan, boil potatoes in water until fork-tender, about 20 minutes; drain and set aside to cool. Combine cheese, mayonnaise, sour cream and onion; mix in potatoes, tossing gently to coat. Spread potato mixture in a buttered 13"x9" baking pan; sprinkle bacon on top. Bake, uncovered, at 350 degrees until golden and bubbly, about 20 to 25 minutes.

Serves 8.

BACON-WRAPPED CORN ON THE COB

LINDA STONE
COOKEVILLE, TN

You can get these tasty morsels ready the night before by refrigerating the ears in plastic zipping bags. Just take them out and toss on the grill...so easy!

Soak corn for about 30 minutes in cold water. Remove corn from water; pull back husks and remove corn silk, leaving husks intact. Wrap 2 slices of bacon around each ear; pull husks back up around corn. Place ears on a hot grill, turning occasionally, until bacon is cooked and corn is tender, about 20 minutes.

8 ears corn, unhusked
1 lb. bacon

Makes 8 servings.

CHAPTER THREE

WORTH SINGIN' ABOUT
Soups & Sandwiches

GATHER 'ROUND THE CAMPFIRE

TOGETHER WITH FAMILY & FRIENDS

TO COZY UP WITH A BOWL OF

HEARTY SOUP OR A TASTY

SANDWICH PERFECT FOR PACKIN' IN

THE SADDLE BAG!

PIONEER BEEF STEW

**ANGIE O'KEEFE
SODDY DAISY, TN**

*There's nothing more satisfying than a hearty bowl of beef stew! It's
baked, not simmered on the stovetop...no need to watch it.*

14-1/2 oz. can petite
  diced tomatoes
1 c. water
3 T. quick-cooking
  tapioca, uncooked
2 t. sugar
1-1/2 t. salt
1/2 t. pepper
1-1/2 lbs. stew beef cubes
3 to 4 potatoes, peeled
  and cubed
4 carrots, peeled and
  thickly sliced
1 onion, diced

In a large bowl, combine tomatoes with juice, water,
tapioca, sugar, salt and pepper. Mix well; stir in
remaining ingredients. Pour into a greased 3-quart
casserole dish. Cover and bake at 375 degrees
for 1-1/2 to 2 hours, until beef and vegetables are
tender.

Serves 4 to 6.

CHICKEN NOODLE GUMBO

**LORRIE SMITH
DRUMMONDS, TN**

*This colorful dish makes enough to feed a whole bunch of hungry folks!
Look for the "gumbo blend" of frozen vegetables at the market.*

Place chicken, broth and tomatoes with juice in
in a large soup pot. Bring to a boil over medium
heat. Reduce heat; simmer 10 minutes. Add frozen
vegetables, uncooked pasta and seasonings. Return
to a boil. Cover and simmer one hour.

Serves 8 to 10.

**2 lbs. boneless, skinless
chicken breasts, cut
into 1-inch cubes**

**4 16-oz. cans chicken
broth**

**15-oz. can diced
tomatoes**

**32-oz. pkg. frozen okra,
corn, celery and
red pepper mixed
vegetables**

**8-oz. pkg. bowtie pasta,
uncooked**

1/2 t. garlic powder

salt and pepper to taste

BBQ SLOPPY JOE SOUP

BETTY LOU WRIGHT
HENDERSONVILLE, TN

This recipe was a happy accident! One day I made vegetable soup. Remembering leftover sloppy Joe sauce in the fridge, I stirred it into the soup. What a hit!

1 lb. ground beef chuck

16-oz. can barbecue Sloppy Joe sauce

10-3/4 oz. can cream of potato soup

10-3/4 oz. can minestrone soup

1-1/4 c. water

15-oz. can light red kidney beans, drained and rinsed

14-1/2 oz. can green beans, drained

15-1/4 oz. can green peas, drained

15-oz. can diced tomatoes, drained

garlic powder and steak seasoning to taste

Garnish: oyster crackers

In a large saucepan over medium heat, brown beef; drain. Stir in Sloppy Joe sauce; heat through. Add remaining ingredients except crackers; simmer until bubbly, about 10 to 15 minutes. Serve with crackers.

Makes 6 to 8 servings.

EASY MEATBALL HOAGIES

DONNA WILSON
MARYVILLE, TN

Really quick & easy! I love meatball subs and this is a great recipe to make at home.

In a saucepan over medium-low heat, combine meatballs and sauce. Cover and cook for about 15 minutes, stirring occasionally, until meatballs are cooked. Meanwhile, blend butter and garlic powder in a small bowl. Partially open rolls; spread cut sides with butter mixture. Place rolls on a baking sheet. Bake, uncovered, at 350 degrees for 10 minutes, or until toasted. To serve, divide meatballs and sauce among rolls; sprinkle with cheese. Bake 8 to 10 minutes.

Serves 4.

12-oz. pkg. frozen
  meatballs
24-oz. jar spaghetti
  sauce
2 T. butter, softened
1/2 t. garlic powder
4 hoagie rolls, split
1/2 c. shredded
  mozzarella cheese

DINNERTIME CONVERSATION

The Gulf Coastal Plain covers the westernmost part of Tennessee. It lies on a fault line and in 1812 was the site of the worst earthquake in the continental United States.

BUFFALO CHICKEN STEW

**LORI HAINES
JOHNSON CITY, TN**

This is really good to make and then freeze in quart bags...just microwave a bag for a quick supper. Don't add the blue cheese until serving. Yummy on a cold night when you don't want to cook.

2 to 3 lbs. boneless chicken tenders

1/2 c. butter, divided

1-1/2 c. celery, chopped and divided

1-1/2 c. onion, chopped and divided

2 t. salt

1 t. pepper

1 c. carrots, peeled and chopped

2 t. garlic powder

4 15-oz. cans navy or Great Northern beans

2 14-1/2 oz. cans petite diced tomatoes

5-oz. bottle buffalo-style hot pepper sauce

1 T. chili powder

1 T. ground cumin

8-oz. bottle blue cheese salad dressing

4-oz. container blue cheese crumbles

In a slow cooker, combine chicken, 1/4 cup butter, 1/2 cup celery, 1/2 cup onion, salt and pepper. Add enough water to cover ingredients. Cover and cook on low setting for 7 hours to overnight, until chicken is tender. Remove chicken to a plate, reserving mixture in slow cooker. Shred chicken and return to slow cooker; set aside. Melt remaining butter in a skillet over medium heat. Add carrots and remaining celery and onion; season with garlic powder. Sauté until vegetables are tender, about 5 minutes. Add sautéed vegetables to slow cooker along with undrained beans and tomatoes, hot sauce and spices. Stir; add enough water to generously cover ingredients. Cover and cook on low setting for 6 to 8 hours, or on high setting for 3 to 4 hours. Shortly before serving time, combine salad dressing and blue cheese in a bowl. Serve bowls of stew topped with a dollop of dressing mixture.

Serves 10.

Tennessee

POOR MAN'S BEEF STEW

SUSAN WILSON
JOHNSON CITY, TN

My mom often made this simple stew for our family, especially during the winter months, with hot buttery cornbread. We always enjoyed it so much...I still do!

Layer vegetables in a slow cooker; add salt and pepper to taste. Crumble browned beef on top; spread soup over beef. Cover and cook on low setting for 6 hours, or on high setting for 4 hours.

Makes 6 servings.

6 potatoes, peeled and quartered

3 carrots, peeled and diced

1 onion, coarsely chopped

salt and pepper to taste

1 lb. ground beef, browned and drained

10-3/4 oz. can tomato soup

JUST FOR FUN

Clingman's Dome is Tennessee's highest point.

TUSCAN TOMATO SOUP

CAROL HICKMAN
KINGSPORT, TN

My family likes to eat this soup when the weather turns cool. We curl up under blankets and sofa throws while watching a good movie together. Serve this with your favorite sandwich (it's delicious with grilled cheese!) or with bread or cheese sticks.

2 26-oz. cans tomato soup

12-oz. can evaporated milk

1-1/4 c. water

14-1/2 oz. can Italian-seasoned petite diced tomatoes

14-1/2 oz. can diced tomatoes with garlic and olive oil

2 T. Tuscan spice blend

1 T. Italian seasoning

1/4 t. red pepper flakes

salt and pepper to taste

1 t. sugar

1/2 c. grated Parmesan cheese

Garnish: additional grated Parmesan cheese

Optional: Italian-seasoned croutons

In a Dutch oven over medium-high heat, combine soup, evaporated milk and water. Whisk well until blended. Add both cans of tomatoes with juice, seasonings and sugar; stir well. Bring to a low boil. Increase heat to medium-low; stir in Parmesan cheese. Simmer for about 20 minutes, stirring occasionally. Top servings with additional Parmesan cheese and croutons, if desired.

Makes 8 to 10 servings.

RING
L
COOKEVILLE
MARYVILLE
JULIET
OAK RIDGE
MORRISTOWN — BRISTOL

SLOW-COOKER ROAST BEEF SANDWICHES

**DEBORAH GRIGGS
LEXINGTON, TN**

This is delicious and can be served with your favorite chips or French fries. Try spooning it on mini buns for easy-to-hold sandwiches.

Whisk dry mixes in hot water; stir in Worcestershire sauce until mixture is smooth. Arrange roast in a slow cooker; pour mixture over the roast. Cover and cook on low setting for 10 to 12 hours. Transfer roast to a platter and shred with 2 forks. Spoon onto buns; top with cheese. If desired, serve remaining juices from slow cooker as dipping sauce for sandwiches.

Makes 8 to 12 servings.

- 1.05-oz. env. Italian salad dressing mix
- 1-oz. env. au jus gravy mix
- 2 c. hot water
- 2 T. Worcestershire sauce
- 2 to 3-lb. beef rump roast
- 8 to 12 buns, split and toasted
- 8-oz. pkg. mozzarella cheese slices

KITCHEN TIP

A new twist on casserole toppers... try crushed veggie, chicken or cheese-flavored crackers combined with fresh or dried herbs and melted butter. Sprinkle on top before baking for a delicious crunch.

DADDY'S POTATO SANDWICHES

**LORRIE SMITH
DRUMMONDS, TN**

*My dad made these for me when I was a little girl. He didn't do much
cooking, so they were always a special treat. When I became a teenager,
I started making them myself as an after-school snack. I still love them
now, years later. Serve with large glasses of iced tea.*

1 to 2 t. oil
**1 potato, peeled and
sliced into thin rounds**
**Optional: 1/2 onion,
sliced**
4 slices white bread
salt and catsup to taste

Heat oil in a cast-iron skillet over medium heat.
Add potato slices; cook until tender and golden on
both sides. Remove to a paper towel-covered plate.
Sauté onion until translucent, if using; remove to
plate. Layer potatoes and onion on 2 bread slices.
Add salt and catsup; top with remaining bread slices.

Serves 2.

DINNERTIME CONVERSATION

No one's sure how Tennessee got its name,
but two Native American villages were
called Tanasi and Tanasqui, which sound
similar to "Tennessee."

PEPPER & ONION BRATS

LORRIE SMITH
DRUMMONDS, TN

I first tried one of these sandwiches at a large outdoor flea market. Now I make them at home and they are always a big hit! With a side of coleslaw or potato salad, they're an easy dinner everyone enjoys.

Heat oil in a large skillet over medium heat. Add onions, peppers and bratwursts. Cover and cook about 5 minutes. Uncover; continue cooking until onions are translucent and golden. Add salt and pepper to taste. Place a brat and some of the onion mixture on each hot dog bun; top generously with mustard.

Makes 6 servings.

1 T. canola oil
2 onions, chopped
2 green peppers, thinly sliced
6 smoked bratwurst sausages
salt and pepper to taste
6 hot dog buns, split
Garnish: mustard

EASY CHICKEN CHILI

MARY LITTLE
FRANKLIN, TN

Our family loves to enjoy this dish on a chilly Tennessee evening.

2 to 3 5-oz. cans chicken
3 15-oz. cans Great
Northern beans
2 15-1/2 oz. cans hominy
16-oz. jar salsa
2 8-oz. pkgs. shredded
Monterey Jack cheese

Combine all ingredients in a slow cooker, including liquid from cans. Cover and cook on low setting for 8 hours.

Serves 8 to 10.

FAST-FIX TOMATO-BASIL SOUP

LYNSEY JACKSON
MARYVILLE, TN

I like to play in the kitchen, or as my mom fondly calls it, "making potion."
This was one of my very successful concoctions and my family requests it
regularly!

4 10-3/4 oz. cans tomato
soup
2-1/2 c. water
1 c. whipping cream
1 T. chicken bouillon
granules
3 T. grated Romano,
Asiago & Parmesan
cheese blend
2 T. dried basil

Add soup to a stockpot over medium heat. Stir in water, whipping cream, bouillon, cheese and basil. Whisk ingredients together and heat through, but do not boil, stirring occasionally.

Serves 4 to 6.

RING
COOKEVILLE
MARYVILLE
JULIET
OAK RIDGE
MORRISTOWN - BRISTOL

FRENCH DIP SANDWICHES

DEBBIE DEVALK
SPRINGFIELD, TN

Serve the savory broth from the slow cooker in small cups for dipping.

Place roast in a slow cooker; add remaining ingredients except rolls. Cover and cook on high setting for 5 to 6 hours. Remove roast from broth; shred with 2 forks and keep warm. Discard bay leaf; serve beef on rolls.

Makes 6 to 8 sandwiches.

3-lb. beef chuck roast, trimmed
2 c. water
1/2 c. soy sauce
1 t. dried rosemary
1 t. dried thyme
1 t. garlic powder
1 bay leaf
3 to 4 whole peppercorns
8 French rolls, split

PRESENTATION

Set up a framed menu to let everyone know that delicious dishes like Great Grandmother's Pot Roast and Aunt Betty's Pudding Cake await!

CHAPTER FOUR

SMOKY MOUNTAIN
Mains

FILL THEM UP WITH A STICK-TO-THE-RIBS MEAL THAT IS FULL OF FLAVOR AND HEARTY ENOUGH TO SATISFY EVEN THE BIGGEST APPETITE.

CHICKEN-BROCCOLI DIVAN

TIFFANY MAYBERRY
HARRIMAN, TN

This is a delightful recipe. I remember my mother cooking it for me when I was a little girl.

2 c. cooked chicken, cubed

16-oz. pkg. frozen broccoli florets, thawed

2 10-3/4 oz. cans cream of chicken soup

3/4 c. mayonnaise

1 t. lemon juice

1/2 c. shredded Cheddar cheese

Place chicken in a greased 13"x9" baking pan. Layer broccoli on top. In a bowl, stir together soup, mayonnaise and lemon juice. Pour soup mixture over broccoli; top with cheese. Bake, uncovered, at 350 degrees for 45 minutes, or until bubbly.

Serves 4.

SUPREME PIZZA CASSEROLE

TASHA PETENZI
GOODLETTSVILLE, TN

This is a great recipe for a potluck dinner or an easy weeknight supper.

16-oz. pkg. rotini pasta, uncooked

2 5-oz. jars pizza sauce

2-1/4 oz. can sliced black olives, drained

4-oz. can sliced mushrooms, drained

1 green pepper, chopped

1 onion, chopped

20 to 30 pepperoni slices

2 c. shredded pizza-blend or Italian-blend cheese

Cook pasta according to package directions; drain. Combine pasta with remaining ingredients except cheese. Transfer to a 13"x9" baking pan; top with cheese. Bake, uncovered, at 425 degrees for 20 to 25 minutes, until cheese is golden and bubbly.

Serves 8 to 10.

CHICKEN & BROCCOLI PUFFS

TASHA PETENZI
GOODLETTSVILLE, TN

This recipe is a super easy, cheesy favorite.

Separate crescent rolls; place one tablespoon chicken in the center of each. Roll up according to package directions. Arrange rolls in a lightly greased 13"x9" baking pan. Mix together soup, milk and cheese; pour over crescent rolls. Bake, uncovered, at 350 degrees for approximately one hour, or until rolls are golden. Spoon cheese sauce from chicken puffs over broccoli and serve together.

Serves 4.

- 10-oz. tube refrigerated crescent rolls
- 2 10-oz. cans chicken, drained
- 10-3/4 oz. can cream of chicken soup
- 1 c. milk
- 8-oz. pkg. shredded Cheddar cheese
- 10-oz. pkg. frozen chopped broccoli, cooked and drained

SALMON CORNBREAD CAKES

**LORRIE SMITH
DRUMMONDS, TN**

A different take on traditional salmon croquettes. I absolutely love these!

2 T. mayonnaise

2 eggs, beaten

1 t. dried parsley

3 green onions, thinly sliced

1 t. seafood seasoning

1 to 2 t. Worcestershire sauce

14-3/4 oz. can salmon, drained and bones removed

2 c. cornbread, crumbled

1 T. canola oil

Combine mayonnaise, eggs, parsley, green onions, seafood seasoning and Worcestershire sauce. Mix well. Mix in salmon and cornbread. Shape into 6 to 8 patties. Heat oil in a skillet over medium heat. Cook patties for 3 to 4 minutes on each side, until golden.

Serves 6.

POT ROAST & DUMPLINGS

WENDY SENSING
BRENTWOOD, TN

This is one of our favorite meals on a chilly day...at the end of a busy day, dinner is practically ready!

Place carrots and potatoes in a slow cooker. Place roast on top; sprinkle with garlic salt and pepper. Stir together water and soup mix; pour over roast. Cover and cook on low setting for 6 to 8 hours. Drain most of broth from slow cooker into a large soup pot; bring to a boil over medium-high heat. Drop dumpling batter into boiling broth by teaspoonfuls. Cover and cook for 15 minutes. Serve dumplings with roast and vegetables.

Dumplings:

Sift together flour, salt and baking powder. Add cream and stir quickly to make a medium-soft batter.

Serves 8 to 10.

2 c. baby carrots

5 potatoes, peeled and halved

4-lb. beef chuck roast

garlic salt and pepper to taste

2 c. water

1-oz. pkg. onion soup mix

DUMPLINGS
2 c. all-purpose flour
1/2 t. salt
3 T. baking powder
1 c. light cream

MAPLE PRALINE CHICKEN

JILL VALENTINE
JACKSON, TN

I have a neighbor who bottles his own maple syrup, and it really makes this dish taste wonderful...so sweet and flavorful!

6 boneless, skinless
  chicken breasts
2 T. Cajun seasoning
1/4 c. butter, melted
1/2 c. maple syrup
2 T. brown sugar,
  packed
1 c. chopped pecans
6-oz. pkg. long-grain
  and wild rice, cooked

Sprinkle chicken with Cajun seasoning. In a skillet over medium- high heat, cook chicken in butter until golden. Arrange chicken in a slow cooker. In a bowl, mix together syrup, brown sugar and pecans; spoon over chicken. Cover and cook on low setting for 6 to 8 hours. Serve with cooked rice.

Serves 6.

Mini Sausage Tarts, p109

Whether you are looking for a quick breakfast to start the day off right, no-fuss party fare for those special guests, satisfying soups and sandwiches for the perfect lunch, main dishes to bring them to the table fast, or a sweet little something to savor at the end of the meal, you'll love these recipes from the amazing cooks in beautiful Tennessee.

Green Tomato Biscuits, p12

PB&J Breakfast Bars, p9

r-Church Egg Muffins, p10

Almond Petit-Fours, p128

Supreme Pizza Casserole, p76

Baked Pancakes with Sausage, p8

Black-Eyed Pea Salad, p39

BBQ Sloppy Joe Soup, p64

Caramel-Filled Chocolate Cookies, p129

Pot Roast & Dumplings, p79

en-Broccoli Divan, p76

Salmon Cornbread Cakes, p78

nch Chicken Pizza, p87

French Dip Sandwiches, p73

Thumbs-Up Cornbread Salad, p38

Tennessee Mud Cake in a Can, p139

Green Bean Bundles, p40

Heat & Hold Scrambled Eggs, p11

Honey-Mustard Spare Ribs, p102

Maple Praline Chicken, p80

Nachos for a Crowd, p108

Granny's Chocolate Cobbler, p127

Pecan Pie Muffins, p57

Pioneer Beef Stew, p62

RANCH CHICKEN PIZZA

LORRIE SMITH
DRUMMONDS, TN

This is my version of a local favorite. Quicker than delivery!

If package directs, bake pizza crusts for a few minutes. In a small bowl, combine Alfredo sauce and salad dressing mix. Divide between 2 crusts, spreading evenly. Top each pizza with 2 cups mozzarella cheese. On each pizza, arrange half of the remaining ingredients except garnish. Sprinkle with Parmesan cheese. Bake at 425 degrees for 20 minutes, or until crust is lightly golden and cheese is bubbly.

Makes 2 pizzas.

- 2 12-inch ready-to-use pizza crusts
- 16-oz. jar Alfredo sauce
- 2-oz. pkg. ranch salad dressing mix
- 4 c. shredded mozzarella cheese, divided
- 8-oz. pkg. grilled chicken strips, coarsely chopped
- 2.8-oz. pkg. ready-to-use bacon, crumbled
- 1 red onion, thinly sliced
- 1 green pepper, sliced into thin strips
- 3 roma tomatoes, thinly sliced
- Garnish: grated Parmesan cheese

GRANDMA'S STUFFED EASTER HAM

BEVERLY STOVALL
LIVINGSTON, TN

This ham was a special dish my mom made for my dad as I was growing up. His mother had fixed it for their large farm family, living in a small Kentucky town. It is so good! When the ham is sliced, it will be marbled with the kale. It is really delicious served hot. It also makes great sandwiches served on rye bread with hot mustard.

8 to 10-lb. uncured (not smoked) ham

1 bunch green onions, diced

salt and pepper to taste

1/2 lb. fresh kale, chopped

Place ham in a roasting pan. Bake, uncovered, at 300 degrees for 2 to 2-1/2 hours. While ham is baking, cover kale and onions with water in a saucepan; season with salt and pepper. Bring to a boil over medium heat; reduce heat to low and simmer for 20 to 25 minutes, until tender. Drain and set aside. Remove ham from oven; score ham front to back, fairly deeply, in several places. Press kale mixture into the scored cuts, packing fairly tightly. Use wooden toothpicks to hold ham together, as needed. Bake, uncovered, for another 2 to 2-1/2 hours. Remove to a serving platter; let stand for 10 to 15 minutes before slicing.

Serves 8 to 10.

OVEN-BARBECUED CHICKEN

PAULA EGGLESTON
KNOXVILLE, TN

When we have company over, this is a great recipe to double. There's always plenty. I serve this yummy chicken with yellow rice and spoon some extra sauce over both.

In a saucepan over medium heat, melt butter. Add onion; cook and stir until tender. Add remaining ingredients except chicken. Heat to boiling; reduce heat and simmer for 10 minutes, stirring occasionally. Arrange chicken pieces in an ungreased 13"x9" baking pan; spoon butter mixture over top. Bake, uncovered, at 350 degrees for one hour and 15 minutes, or until juices run clear when chicken is pierced.

Serves 4.

2 T. butter
1 onion, sliced
1/4 c. water
2 T. brown sugar, packed
1 T. Worcestershire sauce
1 c. catsup
1/4 t. garlic powder
1 t. salt
1/4 t. pepper
3 to 3-1/2 lbs. chicken

KATHY'S CHICKEN CREATION

KATHY GREEVER
MOUNTAIN CITY, TN

I just tossed together some ingredients and came up with this... it is delicious! This freezes well, or leftovers make a great lunch the next day.

16-oz. pkg. rotini pasta or elbow macaroni, uncooked

16-oz. container cottage cheese

2 c. grated Parmesan cheese

2 t. water

8-oz. jar mild salsa

16-oz. pkg. grilled and carved chicken breast, cut into bite-size pieces

2 c. Alfredo sauce

8-oz. pkg. shredded Cheddar cheese

1/8 t. salt

1/8 t. pepper

Cook pasta according to package directions; drain. Meanwhile, combine cottage cheese, Parmesan cheese and water in a bowl; stir well and set aside. In a greased 13"x9" baking pan: layer 1/3 each of cooked pasta, cottage cheese mixture, salsa, chicken, Alfredo sauce and Cheddar cheese. Repeat layering twice, adding salt and pepper before adding Cheddar cheese. Bake, uncovered, at 350 degrees for 20 to 25 minutes, until hot and bubbly.

Serves 8.

ITALIAN CHICKEN SPAGHETTI

LYDIA EDGY
KNOXVILLE, TN

My best friend, Jenny, shared this with me. We no longer live close to one another, but every time I make this I think of her.

Place bread crumbs into a large plastic zipping bag. Moisten chicken with a little water and place into bag with crumbs; shake until chicken is coated. Heat oil in a large skillet over medium heat. Add chicken to skillet; cook until golden and juices run clear. While chicken is cooking, boil spaghetti in broth for 8 to 10 minutes, until tender; drain. Serve chicken over spaghetti, sprinkled with Parmesan cheese.

Serves 4.

1 c. Italian-flavored dry bread crumbs

4 boneless, skinless chicken breasts, halved

2 t. olive oil

16-oz. pkg. spaghetti, uncooked

4 c. chicken broth

Garnish: grated Parmesan cheese

DINNERTIME CONVERSATION

The earliest inhabitants of Tennessee are believed to have been Ice Age peoples descended from Asians who crossed the former Bering Strait land bridge more than 20,000 years ago.

BUTTER-ROASTED CHICKEN

STEPHANIE MONROE
FRANKLIN, TN

You'll love this savory golden chicken...it takes very little effort to prepare.

10 bone-in chicken
  thighs
1 c. water
1/2 c. lemon juice
2 T. butter, sliced
2 T. paprika
2 t. brown sugar, packed
2 t. salt
1 t. pepper
1 t. dried rosemary
1 t. chicken bouillon
  granules
1/4 t. cayenne pepper
1/4 t. nutmeg

Place chicken in an ungreased 13"x9" baking pan; set aside. Combine remaining ingredients in a small saucepan. Bring to a boil over medium-high heat; boil and stir for 2 minutes. Spoon mixture over chicken. Cover with aluminum foil; bake at 325 degrees for one hour. Uncover; baste chicken with pan drippings. Increase oven temperature to 450 degrees. Bake, uncovered, an additional 20 minutes, or until chicken is crisp and golden, about 20 more minutes.

Serves 5.

PRESENTATION

Make it easy for guests to mingle and chat...set up food at several tables instead of one big party buffet. Place hot foods on one table, chilled foods on another, sweets on yet another.

ROY'S STEAK SEASONING

**LINDA RICH
BEAN STATION, TN**

One day I was surprised to find that our favorite steak seasoning was no longer being made. I experimented and created this seasoning mix. My husband said he couldn't tell the difference! It's delicious on just about anything, even beef stew. We've given jars of it to friends for Christmas gifts. They love it and hint often for refills!

In a food processor, finely chop onion to same consistency as other ingredients. Combine all ingredients in a bowl; mix well. Store in airtight containers. To use, sprinkle to taste over steak, burgers, chicken and pork loin while grilling. For a smaller quantity, measure with tablespoons instead of cups.

1 c. dried, minced onion
1 c. granulated garlic
4 c. kosher salt
1 c. paprika
1 c. coarse pepper

Makes 7 cups.

OH-SO-GOOD CRISPY CHICKEN

BETTY LOU WRIGHT
HENDERSONVILLE, TN

I fix this chicken once a week. Not only is it easy to prepare, it fills the house with a wonderful aroma of garlic and cheese. Leftovers are delicious cubed and served on salad greens. Very, very good!

1/4 c. margarine
1/2 c. Italian-flavored dry bread crumbs
1/4 t. garlic powder
1/4 c. grated Parmesan cheese
4 boneless, skinless chicken breasts

Melt margarine in a small saucepan over low heat. Stir in garlic powder and Parmesan cheese. Dip chicken in margarine mixture; arrange in an ungreased 9"x9" baking pan. Sprinkle bread crumbs on top. Bake, uncovered, at 350 degrees for one to 1-1/2 hours, until golden and chicken juices run clear when pierced.

Makes 4 servings.

RUBY SAUCE

JILL VALENTINE
JACKSON, TN

Sweet, tart and absolutely the best sauce...you really have to try it on ribs, chicken or pulled pork!

1 c. brown sugar, packed
1 c. sugar
1 c. cider vinegar
1 t. ground ginger
1 t. cinnamon
1 t. allspice
1 t. paprika
1/2 t. ground cloves
1/2 t. red pepper akes
1/2 t. salt
1/8 t. pepper
2 onions, finely chopped
4 c. rhubarb, finely chopped

Combine all ingredients except onions and rhubarb in a large saucepan over medium heat. Bring to a simmer; stir in onions and rhubarb. Cook for 45 minutes to one hour, until thickened and rhubarb is tender.

Serves 4 to 6.

AUTUMN APPLE-CHEDDAR CHICKEN

SARAH CAMERON
MARYVILLE, TN

This is an awesome, heartwarming fall dish that's savory and sweet. Serve with fresh carrots and broccoli and you have a meal the whole family will love.

Place chicken in a large pot of boiling water. Cook for 8 to 10 minutes; set aside. Combine cracker crumbs with 1/2 cup butter; mix thoroughly. Add remaining butter to a saucepan; stir in flour and cook about one minute, stirring often. Add milk, soup and cheese; stir to blend until cheese is melted. Place chicken in a greased 13"x9" baking pan. Cover chicken with cheese sauce, top with sliced apples and sprinkle with cracker mixture. Bake, covered, at 350 degrees for 35 to 40 minutes.

Makes 6 servings.

5 to 6 boneless, skinless chicken breasts

2 sleeves round buttery crackers, crushed

1/2 c. plus 3 T. butter, melted

1/4 c. all-purpose flour

3/4 c. milk

10-3/4 oz. can Cheddar cheese soup

1 c. shredded Cheddar cheese

3 Golden Delicious apples, cored and sliced

CHEESY HAM BAKE

BETTY LOU WRIGHT
HENDERSONVILLE, TN

This casserole is comforting and delicious. My family enjoys it on Christmas Eve, and it's good for brunch the next morning too... if there's any left! Sometimes for a change I use half mozzarella cheese and half Cheddar cheese.

12 slices Italian or French bread, divided

1 to 1-1/2 c. cooked ham, diced

2 c. shredded mozzarella cheese, divided

3 eggs, beaten

2 c. milk

1/4 to 1/2 c. onion, chopped

garlic salt and pepper to taste

Arrange 6 bread slices in a lightly greased 13"x9" baking pan. Sprinkle with ham and one cup cheese; top with remaining bread. In a bowl, stir together eggs, milk, onion and seasonings; pour over bread. Bake, uncovered, at 350 degrees for 40 minutes. Sprinkle with remaining cheese; bake an additional 5 minutes. Let stand 5 minutes before serving.

Serves 8 to 10.

KING
COOKEVILLE
JULIET
OAK RIDGE
MARYVILLE
MORRISTOWN — BRISTOL

NICE & SPICY PORK RIBS

**CAROL HICKMAN
KINGSPORT, TN**

This is a nice and easy, and delicious, Sunday dinner. I usually toss these ribs in the slow cooker before leaving for Sunday morning service. Back home after church, I can quickly put together some baked beans, corn on the cob, hot dinner rolls, and if I'm feeling especially generous, a peach cobbler for dessert.

Add both bottles of barbecue sauce to a 5-quart slow cooker; cover and turn to high setting. Season ribs with salt and pepper. Heat oil in a large cast-iron skillet over medium-high heat. Add ribs; brown on both sides, but do not cook through. (For even more flavor, use a hot grill for this step.) Drain ribs on paper towels for several minutes; transfer to slow cooker. Spoon sauce in slow cooker over ribs. Cover and cook on high setting for 3 hours, or on low setting for 4 hours. Uncover for the last hour to allow sauce to thicken.

Serves 4 to 6.

19-oz. bottle spicy original barbecue sauce

18-oz. bottle spicy honey barbecue sauce

2 to 2-1/2 lbs. country-style boneless pork ribs

salt and pepper to taste

1 T. oil

CHEESEBURGER MEATBALLS

SHEILA GWALTNEY
JOHNSON CITY, TN

My kids eat these meatballs without one complaint...adults like them too! Once I even made 200 servings for a wedding I catered and everyone raved about them.

1/2 c. pasteurized process cheese sauce
1/4 c. catsup
1/2 c. milk or water
12-1/2 oz. pkg. frozen beef or turkey meatballs
Optional: 1/2 c. onion, chopped
cooked rice or pasta

Mix cheese sauce, catsup and milk or water in a skillet. Bring to a boil over medium heat. Stir in meatballs and onion, if using. Reduce heat to medium-low. Simmer for 15 minutes, stirring occasionally, until sauce is thickened. Serve over rice or pasta.

Serves 4.

KITCHEN TIP

A pat of homemade garlic butter really adds flavor to warm bread or steamed vegetables. Blend equal parts of softened butter and olive oil, then stir in finely chopped garlic to taste...so easy!

CREAMED CHICKEN OVER CORNBREAD

BOBBI GREENE
MOUNT JULIET, TN

This delicious, quick recipe helped stretch the family food budget when our daughter was young and I was a stay-at-home mom. For a change, serve over warm, split biscuits.

Prepare and bake cornbread mix according to package directions. While cornbread is baking, combine chicken and water in a saucepan. Cook over medium-low heat until chicken is very tender, about 15 minutes; drain. In a separate saucepan, mix soup, milk and pepper; cook over medium heat until hot and creamy. Add chicken to soup mixture and stir to coat; heat through. Cut baked cornbread into squares. Split cornbread squares and top with chicken mixture.

Serves 2 to 4.

8-1/2 oz. pkg. cornbread mix

2 boneless, skinless chicken breasts, cut into bite-size pieces

2/3 c. water

10-3/4 oz. can cream of chicken soup

1 c. milk

1/2 t. pepper

STUFFED CUBE STEAKS

**JUDITH LONG
HARRIMAN, TN**

*This is a recipe that I have made for years...my family loves it!
Just add a veggie and voilà, a quick & easy meal.*

6-oz. pkg. stuffing mix
4 beef cube steaks
0.87-oz. pkg. brown
  gravy mix
2 to 3 t. oil

Prepare stuffing mix according to package directions, adding a little extra liquid to make it extra moist. Place a heaping spoonful of stuffing on each steak; roll up and secure with wooden toothpicks. Place oil in a large cast-iron skillet over medium-high heat; add stuffed steaks and brown on all sides. Meanwhile, prepare gravy mix according to package directions. When steaks are browned on all sides, add gravy to skillet. Reduce heat; cover and simmer for about 10 minutes, until steaks are tender.

Serves 4.

MACARETTI

**INGRID BUTTERMORE
CUMBERLAND CITY, TN**

*My parents had eight children. They needed fast, inexpensive suppers
that would go a long way. This dish fits the bill! Serve with a vegetable
or green salad and garlic bread for a complete meal.*

7-1/4 oz. pkg. macaroni
  & cheese mix
10-3/4 oz. can tomato
  soup
1 lb. ground beef,
  chicken, turkey or
  sausage

Prepare macaroni & cheese mix according to package directions. In a skillet, brown meat over medium-high heat; drain. Add macaroni & cheese and soup to skillet. Stir well; heat through. Serve immediately.

Serves 4.

POOR MAN'S LOBSTER

LINDA STONE
SMITHVILLE, TN

For the mildest tasting, most tender monkfish, choose lighter colored fillets. If you like, use olive oil for baking, then butter for dipping.

Arrange fish fillets in a lightly greased shallow 13"x9" baking pan. Drizzle half of melted butter over fish; sprinkle with seasonings to taste. Add a little lemon zest to remaining butter; set aside and keep warm. Bake fish, uncovered, at 375 degrees for 15 to 25 minutes, until fish flakes easily with a fork. Garnish as desired; serve with warm lemon butter for dipping.

Makes 4 servings.

- 1-1/2 lbs. monkfish fillets
- 1 c. butter, melted and divided
- salt, pepper and paprika to taste
- lemon zest to taste
- Garnish: lemon slices, fresh parsley sprigs

YUMMY PORK & GRAVY

CINDY SULLIVAN
SHELBYVILLE, TN

While rice is a good go-with for these pork chops too, cornbread makes a really tasty change.

Combine all ingredients except cornbread in a slow cooker; mix well. Cover and cook on low setting for 6 hours, or on high setting for 4 hours. Serve over cornbread.

Makes 8 servings.

- 6 boneless pork chops, cut into bite-size pieces
- 2 10-3/4 oz. cans cream of mushroom soup
- 6-oz. can French fried onions
- 2 stalks celery, chopped
- 1-1/4 c. milk
- 1-1/2 t. salt
- 1 t. Pepper
- cornbread

HONEY-MUSTARD SPARERIBS

MEGAN BROOKS
ANTIOCH, TN

You'll love this lip-smacking sauce that's made from just a few pantry ingredients. Cut the spareribs into single ribs for yummy finger food, or into 4-rib sections for dinner. If the weather is nice, grill the microwaved ribs over hot coals instead of broiling.

1/2 c. teriyaki marinade
   & sauce
2 T. honey
4 t. Dijon mustard
1 t. garlic powder
3 lbs. pork spareribs,
   cut into serving-size
   portions

Combine all ingredients except spareribs in a large bowl; mix well. Add spareribs; toss until well coated with sauce. Arrange ribs meat-side up in a microwave-safe glass baking pan; reserve sauce in bowl. Let ribs stand 10 minutes. Cover with plastic wrap. Microwave on medium-high setting for 16 minutes, rotating dish once. Place ribs on a broiler pan; brush with remaining sauce. Place 4 to 5 inches under preheated broiler. Broil for 5 to 6 minutes on each side, brushing once with remaining sauce, until browned.

Makes 4 to 6 servings.

DINNERTIME CONVERSATION

What is now Tennessee was initially part of North Carolina, and later part of the Southwest Territory. Tennessee was admitted to the Union as the 16th state on June 1, 1796.

GRANNY'S GRAVY CHICKEN

DIANE CARTER
CAMDEN, TN

My mother-in-law Frances Rich Carter prepared this delicious chicken almost every Sunday when we all gathered at her house after church for lunch. I know she was making it in the 1960s and I think the addition of barbecue sauce was her idea. I now make it for my husband & myself. We always have creamed potatoes with it and use the extra gravy on them.

Combine all ingredients except chicken and flour in a deep 3-quart casserole dish. Mix well; bring to a boil in the oven at 350 degrees, or heat in the microwave. Meanwhile, place chicken in a large plastic zipping bag; add flour. Close bag and shake until well coated. Add chicken to boiling liquid. Sprinkle any extra flour from bag over chicken. Spoon hot liquid over flour until all moistened. If there is not enough liquid, add a little hot water. Bake, uncovered, at 350 degrees for one to 1-1/2 hours, turning chicken halfway through cooking time. Liquid and flour will turn into gravy. If gravy is getting too thick, add a little more hot water; stir to a smooth consistency.

1-1/2 c. water
1/3 c. white vinegar
1 to 2 T. favorite
  barbecue sauce
1 t. salt
1 t. pepper
3/4 c. shortening, melted
3 to 3-1/2 lbs. chicken
  pieces
1-1/2 c. all-purpose flour

Makes 6 to 8 servings.

GRANDMA'S CHICKEN PASTIES

**CARRIE GERING
MADISONVILLE, TN**

Back in the day, my Grandpa worked in a limestone quarry in Indiana. Before the sun was up, Grandma was up making breakfast for the family. She'd make these for Grandpa's lunch bucket too. Simple and simply delicious! Now we eat these on cold days (or not!) when we want something that'll stick to the ribs and bring back that homestyle feeling. P.S. It's pronounced PASS-ties!

2 c. cooked chicken, cubed

3-oz. pkg. cream cheese, softened

6 to 7 T. butter, melted and divided

2 T. milk

1 T. onion, minced

1 T. chopped pimentos, drained

1/4 t. salt

1/8 t. pepper

8-oz. tube refrigerated crescent rolls

1/2 c. dry bread crumbs or crushed croutons

In a bowl, combine chicken, cream cheese, 3 tablespoons melted butter, milk, onion, pimentos and seasonings. Mix well; mixture should be creamy but not thin. Unroll crescent roll dough. Separate dough into 4 squares; gently press together to seal seam. Spoon 1/2 cup of chicken mixture into the center of each square. Pull in all 4 corners, matching opposite corners diagonally; press gently to seal. Brush tops with remaining melted butter; cover with crumbs. Place pasties on an ungreased baking sheet. Bake at 350 degrees for 25 to 30 minutes, until lightly golden. Serve hot.

Makes 4 to 6 servings.

ANGELA'S TORTILLA STACK

ANGELA CRADIC
KINGSPORT, TN

We like to think of this yummy dish as Mexican lasagna.

Crumble 1/4 of browned beef into the bottom of a slow cooker. Top with 1/4 of tortilla wedges. In a small bowl, blend soup and seasoning mix, using 2/3 to all of seasoning mix as desired. Spread 1/4 of soup mixture over tortillas. Sprinkle with 1/4 of tomatoes. Repeat layering until all ingredients are used. Cover and cook on low setting for 4 to 5 hours. Spoon onto individual plates. Top each serving with sour cream and lettuce as desired.

Makes 4 servings.

1 lb. ground beef, browned and drained

5 to 6 6-inch corn tortillas, each cut into 6 wedges

10-3/4 oz. can Cheddar cheese soup

1-1/4 oz. pkg. taco seasoning mix

2 tomatoes, chopped

Garnish: sour cream, shredded lettuce

SMOKY MOUNTAIN SKILLET

GINGER MARSHALL
LOUISVILLE, TN

Many nights at our family cabin, my mom would make this easy dish that we all loved. I can still see us all now, sitting around that big round oak table, eating this dish with wedges of warm cornbread and ripe red homegrown tomatoes...what a delicious memory!

Heat oil in a skillet; add potatoes, onion, salt and pepper. Cook over medium heat until potatoes are tender and golden. Add roast beef in gravy and mix in well; stir in water. Cover skillet and cook over low heat for 15 to 20 minutes.

Serves 5 to 6.

1/4 c. oil

5 to 6 potatoes, peeled or unpeeled, cubed

1 onion, chopped

salt and pepper to taste

12-oz. can roast beef in gravy

1/2 c. water

CHAPTER FIVE

GRAND OLE OPRY

Appetizers & Snacks

WHETHER YOU ARE HAVING
COMPANY OR JUST NEED A
LITTLE SNACK TO HOLD YOU OVER
UNTIL THE NEXT MEAL, YOU'LL
FIND THESE RECIPES ARE GREAT
FOR TAKING ON-THE-GO OR AS A
FAVORITE APPETIZER.

NACHOS FOR A CROWD

COLLEEN SEATON
NASHVILLE, TN

A real party starter! If you like, substitute 1-1/2 cups of your own homemade chili.

13-1/2 oz. pkg. round tortilla chips

15-oz. can homestyle chili

8-oz. pkg. shredded Mexican-blend cheese

1/2 c. queso sauce

10-oz. pkg. shredded lettuce

1 onion, diced

1 green pepper, chopped

1/2 c. jalapeño pepper, sliced

Optional: 1/2 c. sliced black olives,

4-oz. can diced green chiles

Garnish: 1/2 c. sour cream, 1 tomato, diced, 2 T. dried chives

Arrange chips on a large microwave-safe plate; set aside. Heat chili in a microwave-safe bowl on high setting for one minute; stir. Microwave for another minute; set aside. Sprinkle tortilla chips with cheese; microwave on high setting for 30 seconds. Spoon chili and queso sauce over cheese; sprinkle with lettuce, onion and peppers. Top with black olives and green chiles, if desired. Add a dollop of sour cream; sprinkle with tomato and chives.

Serves 6 to 8.

MINI SAUSAGE TARTS

**WANDA BOYKIN
LEWISBURG, TN**

These look so fancy on an appetizer tray...and your friends will never know how easy they are to make!

Combine sausage, cheese, salad dressing and olives; blend well. Divide among phyllo cups; arrange on ungreased baking sheets. If desired, sprinkle with diced pepper and black olives. Bake at 350 degrees for 10 to 12 minutes.

Makes 5 dozen.

1 lb. ground pork sausage, browned and drained

8-oz. pkg. shredded Mexican-blend cheese

3/4 c. ranch salad dressing

2 T. black olives, chopped

4 pkgs. 15-count frozen mini phyllo cups

Optional: diced red pepper, diced black olives

PRESENTATION

When preparing appetizer trays, consider adding colorful fruits, fresh sprigs of mint and fresh flowers both on the platters and in small vases to make pretty garnishes.

KASSIE'S SWEET TEA

KASSIE FRAZIER
WESTPOINT, TN

There is nothing like a cold glass of iced sweet tea on a summer day in Tennessee! I can never remember a time, growing up, that a big gallon of sweet tea wasn't in my family's refrigerator and I have carried on that tradition with my own family. We love our sweet tea and when we say "sweet tea," we mean sweet!

2-1/2 c. sugar
6 regular or 4 family-size tea bags
2 c. warm water
4 c. boiling water

In a one-gallon jug or pitcher, combine sugar and warm water. Stir until sugar is dissolved; set aside. In a separate container, combine boiling water and tea bags. Let stand for 5 minutes to steep; discard tea bags. Add hot tea to sugar mixture. Fill the rest of the jug or pitcher with cold water; stir well. Cover and chill.

Makes one gallon.

SECRET TRAIL CHEESE BALL

BECCA JONES
JACKSON, TN

A different twist to the cheese ball family! I discovered this in a small-town newspaper as part of someone's Christmas tradition. I have used it many times over the years...guests always ask for the recipe.

8-oz. can crushed pineapple, drained
2 8-oz. pkgs. cream cheese, softened
1/3 c. raisins
1/2 c. chopped dates
1/2 c. chopped pecans
round buttery crackers

Mix together all ingredients except pecans and crackers; blend well. Shape into a ball. Roll in chopped pecans. Refrigerate until serving time. Serve with crackers.

Serves 10.

PINKY WINKS

LINDA KNOX
NIOTA, TN

This old-time recipe freezes well...very handy when you're preparing for a large holiday buffet.

In a large skillet over medium heat, cook sausage and beef until browned, breaking up with a spatula. Drain; reduce heat to low. Add remaining ingredients except bread. Cook until cheese is melted, stirring often. Spread warm mixture thinly on bread slices. Arrange slices on ungreased baking sheets. Broil until bubbly and golden, watching carefully.

To Freeze:

Spread sausage mixture on bread slices; place on baking sheets and freeze. Remove frozen slices to plastic zipping bags; keep frozen. To serve, thaw in the refrigerator; broil as directed above.

Serves 8 to 10.

1 lb. hot ground pork sausage

1 lb. ground beef

16-oz. pkg. pasteurized process cheese spread, cubed

4-oz. can sliced mushrooms, drained and diced

1 t. dried oregano

1 t. dried basil

1 t. garlic salt

1/4 t. pepper

1 t. Worcestershire sauce

2 loaves party rye bread

JUST FOR FUN

Tennessee has over 82,000 farms, roughly 59 percent of which accommodate beef cattle.

BROWN SUGAR HOT TEA

MEGAN BROOKS
ANTIOCH, TN

My granddaughter feels so grown-up when I share a pot of this special tea with her. I've found the brown sugar low-calorie sweetener works well with it also.

6 c. boiling water
1/2 c. brown sugar, packed
6 tea bags
Optional: milk or cream

Pour boiling water over tea bags into a teapot and cover. Steep for 5 minutes. Remove tea bags and discard. Stir in brown sugar; add a splash of milk or cream, if desired.

Makes 6 servings.

DONNA'S MANGO SALSA

DONNA WILSON
MARYVILLE, TN

My very picky kids tried this salsa and surprise...they loved how it tasted! If it can please Holly, Matthew, Stacia, Kyra and Adriana, it'll please your picky kids too.

1 mango, peeled, pitted and diced
1 red pepper, diced
1 to 2 jalapeño peppers, seeded and minced
1 red onion, diced
zest and juice of 1 lime
1/2 t. chili lime rub
1/2 t. salt
tortilla chips

Combine all ingredients except tortilla chips in a bowl; mix well. If a smoother texture is desired, transfer mixture to a blender; process to desired consistency. Serve with tortilla chips.

Makes 4 to 6 servings.

BACON ROLL-UPS

BARBARA SHEETS
JOHNSON CITY, TN

A friend at church gave me this easy and delicious recipe.

Prepare stuffing as directed on package. For each roll-up, spoon 2 teaspoons stuffing into each half-slice of bacon; roll up and secure with a wooden toothpick. Place roll-ups on a baking sheet coated with non-stick vegetable spray. Bake at 425 degrees for 30 to 40 minutes, or until bacon is fully cooked, but not crisp. Drain roll-ups on paper towels for about one minute. Transfer to a serving platter; serve immediately.

Makes about 2 dozen.

6-oz. pkg. chicken-flavor stuffing mix
1 lb. bacon, slices cut in half

PARTY BREAD STRIPS

TENA HUCKLEBY
MORRISTOWN, TN

This recipe is great all through the year, for parties and to serve with soup. Save the bread crusts to make croutons.

Cut each bread slice into 3 strips. Place bread strips on an ungreased 14" round pizza pan; set aside. In a bowl, combine mayonnaise and soup mix; spread on bread strips. Top with remaining ingredients. Bake at 350 degrees for 10 minutes, or until cheese is melted. Serve warm.

Makes 21 pieces.

7 slices sandwich bread, crusts removed
2 c. light mayonnaise
1.35-oz. pkg. onion soup mix
1/2 c. shredded low-fat Cheddar cheese
1/4 c. green olives with pimentos, drained and diced
2 T. dried parsley
2 T. pepper

SUMMERTIME CITRUS TEA

**SUSAN WILSON
JOHNSON CITY, TN**

Try herbal tea bags if you like...they'll be just as terrific.

4 c. water
6 tea bags
1-1/2 c. sugar
6-oz. can frozen orange juice concentrate, thawed
6-oz. can frozen lemonade concentrate, thawed
10 c. cold water
ice cubes

Bring water to a boil in a saucepan. Remove from heat and add tea bags; steep overnight. Discard tea bags. Pour into a large pitcher; add remaining ingredients. Serve in tall glasses over ice.

Makes 6 servings.

KNOB CREEK LEMONADE

**KASSIE FRAZIER
WEST POINT, TN**

I've always loved ice-cold lemonade, and my two girls enjoy setting up their own little lemonade stand. So I was ecstatic when my mother-in-law gave me her very own best-ever lemonade recipe!

3 c. sugar
6 lemons, halved
12 c. cold water, divided
ice cubes

Add sugar and 2 cups water to a one-gallon pitcher; stir and let stand. Squeeze lemon halves into pitcher; add 4 or 5 of the lemon halves to pitcher. Add remaining water; stir until sugar is dissolved. Chill; serve over ice.

Makes one gallon.

MIXED-UP OLIVE DIP

LORI HAINES
JOHNSON CITY, TN

My family and I absolutely love olives! Pitted ones, unpitted ones, black, green, stuffed, unstuffed...you name it. My siblings and I are always looking for a new olive dish to introduce. I found this olive dip recipe recently and it turned out wonderfully. I hope that your olive-loving gang will love it as much as mine does.

Combine all ingredients except oil and dippers in a food processor. Pulse until olives and celery are finely minced. Stir in oil. Transfer to a serving bowl. Cover and refrigerate for 4 hours to overnight. Serve with assorted dippers. Also can be used as a sandwich spread or tapenade.

Serves 10.

5-1/4 oz. jar green olives with pimentos, drained

6-oz. can black olives, drained

2 stalks celery, sliced into 2-inch pieces

1 t. onion powder

1 t. Italian seasoning

2 t. garlic, minced

1/4 c. extra-virgin olive oil

assorted dippers such as French bread slices, Melba toast, crackers and raw veggies

KITCHEN TIP

A jar of dried, minced onion can be a real timesaver! If the recipe has a lot of liquid, such as soups and stews, it's easy to switch. Just substitute one tablespoon of dried, minced onion for every 1/3 cup fresh diced onion.

LEMONY-FRESH DILL DIP

LISA BLUMBERG
KNOXVILLE, TN

Enjoy this refreshing dip like we do...by dunking blanched fresh green beans in it. Yummy!

1 c. plain low-fat yogurt
1 T. lemon juice
1/3 c. fresh dill, chopped
salt and pepper to
taste
1 t. lemon zest

Combine all ingredients in a bowl; stir well. Cover and chill before serving.

Makes 4 servings.

FORT WORTH BEAN DIP

BETTY LOU WRIGHT
HENDERSONVILLE, TN

When our son moved to Texas, we were introduced to some mighty fine Tex-Mex cooking. I make this tasty dip when he comes home, just so he won't miss all the good eatin' in Fort Worth. Use low-fat products if you like. Serve with nacho tortilla chips...delicious!

15-oz. can refried beans
1 bunch green onions,
chopped
1-1/2 c. sour cream
1/2 c. cream cheese,
softened
1-1/4 oz. pkg. taco
seasoning mix, or to
taste
1 c. shredded Cheddar
cheese

Combine all ingredients except cheese in a lightly greased 2-quart casserole dish. Sprinkle cheese on top. Bake, uncovered, at 300 degrees for 45 minutes, or until hot and bubbly.

Makes 12 servings.

PUMPKIN CHEESE BALL

CAREY NEBLETT
PLEASANT VIEW, TN

I made this at my very first Halloween party...it looks just like a real pumpkin!

Combine all ingredients except broccoli and crackers. Shape mixture to resemble a pumpkin. Trim broccoli stalk, if needed, and press lightly into the top of the pumpkin for a stem. Use a knife to make vertical lines down the sides of the cheese ball. Serve with crackers.

Serves 10 to 15.

2 8-oz. pkgs. shredded extra sharp Cheddar cheese
8-oz. pkg. cream cheese, softened
8-oz. container chive and onion cream cheese, softened
2 t. paprika
1/2 t. cayenne pepper
1 stalk broccoli, top removed
assorted crackers

FABULOUS FRUIT TEA

BECCA JONES
JACKSON, TN

This fruit tea is so refreshing...it's the best fruit tea I have ever tasted or served! Garnish with an orange slice on the rim of each glass for added appeal.

Bring 4 cups water to a boil in a saucepan over high heat. Stir in sugar until dissolved. Remove from heat; add tea bags. Let stand for 8 to 10 minutes to steep; discard tea bags. Pour tea mixture into a large pitcher. Stir in juices and remaining water. Cover and chill; serve over ice.

Makes 18 servings.

12 c. water, divided
1 c. sugar
9 tea bags
12-oz. can frozen lemonade concentrate, thawed
12-oz. can frozen orange juice concentrate, thawed
3 c. pineapple juice

NASHVILLE HOT BBQ CHICKEN STRIPS

BENNIE WOOD
NASHVILLE, TN

This is a tasty change from hot wings...you'll love it!

1 lb. boneless, skinless chicken breasts, cut into 1/2-inch strips
1/3 c. all-purpose flour
4 T. oil, divided
1/3 c. barbecue sauce
1 T. hot pepper sauce
1/4 c. butter

In a large plastic zipping bag, toss chicken strips with flour. Shake to remove any extra flour; set aside. Heat 2 tablespoons oil in a large skillet over medium-high heat. Add half of chicken strips. Cook for 2 to 3 minutes per side, until golden and juices run clear; drain well. Repeat with remaining oil and chicken strips. Meanwhile, stir together sauces and melted butter in a large bowl. Add cooked chicken; toss to coat.

Serves 4.

ANNIVERSARY PUNCH

LORRIE OWENS
MUNFORD, TN

This punch was served at my grandparents' 50th wedding anniversary celebration on February 16, 1974. I don't recall if I drank any or not...I was only 4 years old at the time! This recipe was originally called Christmas Punch, but I changed the name because I found the recipe in Grandma's recipe box. It had a note at the bottom that said "Serve at anniversary party."

12-oz. can frozen lemonade concentrate
12-oz. can frozen orange juice concentrate
46-oz. can pineapple juice
4 0.13-oz. pkgs. unsweetened cherry drink mix
2-1/2 c. sugar
3 ltrs. ginger ale, chilled

In a punch bowl, prepare frozen juice concentrates, adding water as called for in package directions. Add remaining ingredients except ginger ale. Cover and chill. Add ginger ale a few minutes before serving.

Makes 20 servings.

MAWMAW'S HOT CRACKERS

KASSIE FRAZIER
WEST POINT, TN

Whenever our family has a get-together, our sweet little-bitty MawMaw makes everyone's favorite hot crackers! They go fabulously with her spinach dip. And what's even better, they are a cinch to make! Fat-free saltines are the best at soaking up the oil.

Combine seasonings and salad dressing mix in a gallon-size plastic zipping bag; shake until well blended. Pour oil into bag, followed by crackers; shake until crackers are well coated. Remove from bag; spread on wax paper and allow to dry. Store in an airtight container.

Makes about 6 dozen.

1/2 t. pepper
1 t. red pepper flakes
1 t. cayenne pepper
1-oz. pkg. ranch salad dressing mix
3/4 c. canola oil
2 sleeves fat-free saltine crackers

CHIEF KELLY'S BEAN DIP

RONDA MORHAIME
ROGERSVILLE, TN

I have had this recipe for over 30 years...when I was in the US Navy, my supervisor shared it with me. My family clamors for it at every get-together.

Brown beef in a skillet over medium heat; drain. Combine beef and remaining ingredients in a slow cooker; stir to mix well. Cover and cook on high setting, stirring occasionally, for 4 hours, or until cheese is melted and dip is mixed. Turn heat to low setting to keep warm. Serve with tortilla chips or corn chips for dipping.

Serves 10 to 12.

1 lb. ground beef chuck
16-oz. pkg. pasteurized process cheese spread, cubed
28-oz. can refried beans
1-1/4 oz. pkg. taco seasoning mix
1-1/2 c. salsa

SWEET-AND-SOUR SAUSAGE BALLS

DRUSILLA SMITH
ELIZABETHTON, TN

Add a little chopped garlic to the meatball mixture for extra flavor.

2 lbs. sage-flavored
  ground pork sausage
4 slices bread, toasted
  and crumbled
1 egg, beaten
1/2 c. onion, chopped
8-oz. can pineapple
  chunks
1-1/4 c. catsup
1/2 c. brown sugar,
  packed
1 T. low-sodium soy
  sauce
1 T. lemon juice

In a bowl, mix together sausage, bread crumbs, egg and onion; mix well. Shape sausage mixture into walnut-size balls. Brown meatballs on all sides in a skillet over medium heat. Place meatballs in a slow cooker; set aside. In a bowl, mix together undrained pineapple and remaining ingredients; spoon over meatballs. Cover and cook on high setting for 3 to 4 hours, until meatballs are no longer pink in the center.

Serves 10 to 12.

MINI HAM & CHEESEWICHES

ELISA THOMPSON
CELINA, TN

I always take these little sandwiches to family gatherings. I have a very large family, so I have to make lots!

17-oz. pkg. brown &
  serve dinner rolls
8-oz. pkg. sliced deli
  ham
12 slices American
  cheese
Garnish: melted butter,
  garlic salt

Slice each roll in half like a hamburger bun. Place a slice of ham and a slice of cheese on each roll bottom. Add tops; brush with butter and sprinkle with garlic salt. Arrange on an ungreased baking sheet. Bake at 450 degrees until golden and cheese is melted.

Makes one dozen.

AVOCADO DEVILED EGGS

SARAH CAMERON
MARYVILLE, TN

A different twist on an old favorite, a little healthier and oh-so easy!

Cut eggs in half lengthwise; scoop out yolks into a bowl. Place egg whites on a platter; set aside. In a bowl, mash egg yolks with remaining ingredients. Spoon filling into egg whites. Chill.

Makes one dozen.

6 eggs, hard-boiled and peeled
1 avocado, halved, pitted and cubed
1 t. lemon juice
salt and pepper to taste

GARLICKY CHICKEN BITES

MEGAN BROOKS
ANTIOCH, TN

Yummy and easy to fix...maybe you should make a double batch!

Place chicken in a shallow dish; set aside. In a cup, combine olive oil, garlic and pepper; drizzle over chicken. Turn to coat; cover and refrigerate for 30 minutes. Drain. Combine bread crumbs and cayenne pepper in a separate shallow dish; add chicken cubes and coat well. Arrange on a greased baking sheet in a single layer. Bake at 475 degrees for 10 to 15 minutes, until golden and chicken juices run clear.

Makes 4 servings.

2 boneless skinless chicken breasts, cut into bite-size cubes
1/2 c. olive oil
4 cloves garlic, minced
1/4 t. pepper
1/2 c. dry bread crumbs
1/4 t. cayenne pepper

SUSIE'S MAKE-AHEAD DOGGY DOGS

SUSAN PAFFENROTH
JOHNSON CITY, TN

A simple appetizer that everyone's sure to love. Try using turkey or chicken hot dogs too.

3 16-oz. pkgs. hot dogs, sliced into 1-inch pieces
18-oz. bottle barbecue sauce
20-oz. can pineapple chunks, drained and juice reserved
1/2 c. brown sugar, packed
1/4 c. apple jelly
1/4 c. grape jelly

Place hot dogs in a slow cooker; set aside. In a saucepan over medium-low heat, combine barbecue sauce, reserved pineapple juice, brown sugar and jellies. Cook, stirring occasionally, until warmed and combined. Add pineapple chunks to hot dogs in slow cooker; spoon sauce over all. Cover and cook on low setting for 3 hours, or until heated through.

Serves 12 to 15.

CRANBERRY MEATBALLS

LESLEIGH ROBINSON
BROWNSVILLE, TN

This is a great appetizer for Christmas or anytime.

28-oz. pkg. frozen meatballs
2 3/4-oz. pkgs. brown gravy mix
2 14-oz. cans whole-berry cranberry sauce
2 T. whipping cream
2 t. Dijon mustard
2 18-oz. bottles barbecue sauce

Place meatballs in a slow cooker. In a bowl, prepare gravy mixes according to package directions; stir in cranberry sauce, cream and mustard. Pour over meatballs; stir. Cover and cook on low setting for 4 to 5 hours, or on high setting for 2 to 3 hours. Before serving, drain gravy mixture; return meatballs to slow cooker to keep warm. Stir in barbecue sauce.

Serves 10 to 12.

KIMMY'S AMAZING BLACK BEAN CHILI-CHEESE DIP

KIM RALSTON
MURFREESBORO, TN

This festive dip is my go-to dip for any get- together! It freezes wonderfully too, so you can make it in advance.

In a skillet over medium heat, brown beef and sausage until crumbled and no longer pink; drain. To a 6 to 7-quart slow cooker, add cheeses, beans and tomatoes with juice. Add beef mixture. Sprinkle with seasoning mixes; stir well. Cover and cook on low setting for 2 hours, stirring every 20 minutes, until cheeses are melted and dip is warmed through. Turn slow cooker to warm setting; serve with dippers.

Serves 24.

1 lb. ground beef

1 lb. ground pork sausage

32-oz. pkg. pasteurized process cheese spread, cubed

8-oz. pkg. cream cheese, cubed

2 15-1/2 oz. cans black beans, drained and rinsed

3 14-1/2 oz. cans fire-roasted diced tomatoes

6 T. taco seasoning mix

1-oz. pkg. fiesta ranch dip mix

assorted dippers, such as tortilla chips, corn chips and cut veggies

CHAPTER SIX

DAVY CROCKETT
Desserts

THERE IS ALWAYS ROOM FOR

DESSERT. SO WHEN YOUR SWEET

TOOTH IS CALLING, THESE SIMPLE

SWEETS ARE THE PERFECT WAY TO

END THE DAY.

KEY LIME POUND CAKE

GAYLE KRIEGER
CORDOVA, TN

If you want a bit of Florida sunshine in your day, this cake will take you there. Just add a summer breeze...enjoy!

- 18-1/2 oz. pkg. yellow cake mix
- 3-1/4 oz. pkg. instant lemon pudding mix
- 4 eggs, beaten
- 1/2 c. plus
- 1/3 c. Key lime juice, divided
- 1/2 c. canola oil
- 2-1/2 c. powdered sugar

In a large bowl, combine dry cake and pudding mixes, eggs, 1/2 cup lime juice and oil. Beat with an electric mixer on medium speed until well mixed, about 2 minutes. Pour batter into a greased and floured Bundt® cake pan. Bake at 325 degrees for 50 to 60 minutes, until top springs back when pressed. Set cake in pan on a wire rack to cool; invert onto a serving plate. For glaze, combine powdered sugar and remaining lime juice; whisk together until smooth. Pierce top of cake with a fork. Brush glaze over cake; allow to absorb glaze. Repeat until all glaze is used.

Serves 10.

CHOCOLATE OATMEAL COOKIES

LESLEIGH ROBINSON
BROWNSVILLE, TN

I've been making these since I was ten years old. They are the simplest cookies I've ever made...you don't even have to bake them!

- 1/3 c. butter, melted
- 2 c. sugar
- 1/2 c. milk
- 1/3 c. baking cocoa
- 1 t. vanilla extract
- 1/2 c. creamy peanut butter
- 3 c. quick-cooking oats, uncooked

In a saucepan over medium heat, combine butter, sugar, milk and cocoa. Bring to a boil; cook for one minute. Remove from heat; stir in remaining ingredients. Mix well; drop by rounded teaspoonfuls onto wax paper. Let cookies cool completely.

Makes about 2 dozen.

GRANNY'S CHOCOLATE COBBLER

LORRIE SMITH
MUNFORD, TN

This recipe has been passed around my family for years. It's just too yummy for words...yet oh-so quick & easy to make!

Spread melted butter in a 13"x9" baking pan; set aside. In a large bowl, combine 1-1/2 cups sugar, flour, milk, 2 tablespoons cocoa and vanilla. Pour over butter in pan. In a small bowl, mix remaining sugar and cocoa; sprinkle evenly over batter. Pour boiling water over batter; do not stir. Bake at 350 degrees for 30 minutes. Serve warm, garnished as desired.

Makes 6 to 8 servings.

3/4 c. butter, melted

3 c. sugar, divided

1-1/2 c. self-rising flour

1/2 c. milk

1/2 c. plus 2 T. baking cocoa, divided

2 t. vanilla extract

2-1/2 c. boiling water

Optional: fresh strawberries, coarse sugar

AUNT PATSY'S PEACH PIE

KASSIE FRAZIER
WEST POINT, TN

My aunt's recipe for peach pie is melt-in-your-mouth good. This recipe has been served at every family gathering for as long as I can remember. And in our large family, you'd better get to this dessert, as we say, while the gettin' is good...otherwise it will be gone!

Spray a 13"x9" baking pan with non-stick vegetable spray; pour melted butter into pan. Cut peach slices into thirds; add peaches with juice to pan and set aside. In a bowl, combine flour, sugar and milk; mix well. Pour batter over peaches; do not stir. Bake at 350 degrees for 50 to 60 minutes, until golden.

Makes 6 servings.

1/2 c. margarine, melted

1-1/2 c. sugar

2 15-oz. cans sliced peaches

1-1/2 c. all-purpose flour

1 c. milk

ALMOND PETIT-FOURS

JILL VALENTINE
JACKSON, TN

The trick to this elegant dessert is stacking mini cupcakes. Tint the frosting with food coloring or garnish with sprinkles for variety.

18-1/4 oz. pkg. yellow
  cake mix
1/2 t. almond extract
3 c. sliced almonds
Garnish: candy-coated
  almonds

ALMOND FROSTING
3 c. powdered sugar
2 t. almond extract
3 T. hot water

In a bowl, prepare cake mix according to package directions, adding almond extract into the batter. Fill paper-lined mini muffin cups 2/3 full. Bake at 350 degrees for 15 to 17 minutes; cool completely on wire racks. Spread Almond Frosting on half the cupcakes; these will be the bottom-layer cupcakes. Remove the liners from the remaining cupcakes and place them upside-down on top of the bottom-layer cupcakes. Frost the top-layer cupcakes on all sides. Coat cupcake sides with sliced almonds. Arrange candy-coated almonds on top.

Almond Frosting:

In a bowl, combine all ingredients. Beat to desired consistency, adding more water or sugar as needed.

Makes about 3 dozen.

CARAMEL-FILLED CHOCOLATE COOKIES

MEGAN BROOKS
ANTIOCH, TN

I loved to help my Grandma Studer bake. She taught me how to make these wonderful cookies!

In a medium bowl, beat brown sugar, one cup sugar and margarine until fluffy. Mix in eggs and vanilla. In another bowl, combine flour, baking soda, cocoa and 1/2 cup pecans; stir into sugar mixture until combined. In a cup, mix remaining pecans and sugar; set aside. For each cookie, shape one tablespoon of dough around one caramel. Dip the dough ball, one side only, into the pecan mixture. Place cookies, pecan mixture-side up, on ungreased baking sheets. Bake at 375 degrees for 7 to 10 minutes. Cool on baking sheets 2 minutes; remove to a wire rack to cool completely.

Makes 4 dozen.

- 1 c. brown sugar, packed
- 1 c. plus 1 T. sugar, divided
- 1 c. margarine, softened
- 2 eggs, beaten
- 2 t. vanilla extract
- 2-1/4 c. all-purpose flour
- 1 t. baking soda
- 3/4 c. baking cocoa
- 1 c. chopped pecans, divided
- 48 chocolate-covered caramels, unwrapped

PRESENTATION

You're never too old for party favors! Send your guests home with a whimsical memento...tiny potted plants, little bags of homemade candy, mini photo frames or even bubbles.

MINT-CHOCOLATE CHIP COOKIES

**AMY BELL
ARLINGTON, TN**

These cookies are so pretty and taste like a bite of Christmas. For make-ahead convenience, shape the dough into balls, freeze them on a baking sheet, and then store them in freezer bags. On baking day, just roll the cookies in the crushed candy and bake for ten minutes.

1/2 c. plus 2 T. butter, softened
1 c. sugar
1 egg, beaten
1/2 t. vanilla extract
1/2 t. peppermint extract
1 c. plus
1 T. all-purpose flour
6 T. baking cocoa
1/2 t. baking soda
1/4 t. salt
1/2 c. mini semi-sweet chocolate chips
3/4 c. peppermint candy canes, crushed

Blend together butter, sugar, egg and vanilla. Beat for 4 minutes, until creamy. In a separate bowl, combine flour, cocoa, baking soda and salt; stir into butter mixture and blend well. Fold in chocolate chips. Scoop dough by teaspoonfuls and roll in crushed candy. Place on lightly greased baking sheets. Bake at 350 degrees for 8 to 9 minutes.

Makes 2 dozen.

KITCHEN TIP

A pinch of ground cloves brings out the flavor in cinnamon-sugar.

SNOWY ICICLES

GAYLE KRIEGER
CORDOVA, TN

My sister used to make cookies every Christmas with Sister Mary Monica at the Ursuline Convent in Toledo, Ohio. We always made candy cane cookies with this recipe, but since we have a lot of January birthdays in my family, I came up with this fun new twist for our winter birthdays.

Blend together one cup butter, 1/2 cup powdered sugar and one teaspoon vanilla. Sift together flour and salt; add half of our mixture to butter mixture. In a separate bowl, blend together remaining butter, sugar and vanilla. Add food coloring; mix well. Add remaining flour mixture to blue dough. Cover and chill dough for 2 hours to overnight. Form a ball with a small amount of white dough; roll into a long rope. Repeat with blue dough. Twist 2 ropes to form an icicle. Place on ungreased baking sheets. Sprinkle with sugar. Bake at 350 degrees for 12 to 14 minutes, until set.

Makes 2 to 3 dozen.

2 c. butter, divided
1 c. powdered sugar, divided
2 t. vanilla extract, divided
4-1/2 c. all-purpose flour, divided
1/2 t. salt, divided
few drops blue food coloring
Garnish: white cake glitter

OLD DOMINION CHESS PIE

CAROL HICKMAN
KINGSPORT, TN

Think of it as chocolate pecan pie...yum!

Mix together all ingredients except pie crust; pour into pie crust. Bake at 400 degrees for 30 minutes. Let cool completely.

Serves 6 to 8.

5 T. baking cocoa
1-1/2 c. sugar
2 eggs, beaten
1/2 c. chopped pecans
1/4 c. butter, melted
1/2 c. evaporated milk
1/2 c. flaked coconut
9-inch pie crust, unbaked

ROSHKY HUNGARIAN CAKES

SHANNON OROS
MCMINNVILLE, TN

*This recipe has been in our Hungarian family for over a hundred years.
With their light sweetness and flaky dough, these cookies are always
a hit! Try using strawberry jam instead of apricot preserves for another
scrumptious taste.*

**4 8-oz. pkgs. cream
cheese, softened
1 c. butter, softened
2 c. all-purpose flour
16-oz. jar apricot
preserves
1/2 lb. nuts, ground**

Combine cream cheese, butter and flour; blend well.
Form into a roll 3 inches in diameter. Wrap in plastic
wrap; place in refrigerator overnight. Slice dough
into one-inch thick slices; roll out to 1/4-inch thick
on a lightly floured surface. Cut into 2-inch squares,
working quickly so dough does not become sticky. To
make filling, mix together preserves and nuts. Place
a teaspoon of filling on each square of dough. Fold
one corner halfway across the square; fold the other
corner over the first fold to form a crescent. Place on
greased baking sheets. Bake at 350 degrees for 15
to 20 minutes, until lightly golden.

Makes about 4 dozen.

TERRY'S BUTTER BRICKLE COOKIES

TERRY LEE
WAVERLY, TN

Most requested at church socials...delicious!

**18-oz. pkg. butter pecan
cake mix
1/2 c. margarine,
softened
8-oz. pkg. toffee baking
bits
2 eggs, beaten**

Mix together all ingredients. Drop by tablespoonfuls
onto greased baking sheets. Bake at 350 degrees
for 9 to 10 minutes.

Makes 3-1/2 to 4 dozen.

COOKIES & VANILLA CREAM FUDGE

MEGAN BROOKS
ANTIOCH, TN

Creamy, crunchy chocolate...divine!

Melt chocolate, condensed milk and salt in a heavy saucepan over low heat; stir until smooth. Remove from heat; stir in cookies. Spread evenly in a greased aluminum foil-lined 8"x8" baking pan. Chill for 2 hours, or until firm. Turn fudge onto cutting board; peel off foil and cut into squares. Store tightly covered at room temperature.

Makes about 3-1/2 dozen.

- 3 6-oz. pkgs. white chocolate chips
- 14-oz. can sweetened condensed milk
- 1/8 t. salt
- 2 c. chocolate sandwich cookies, coarsely crushed

BLIZZARD PARTY MIX

ELIZABETH MCCORD
BARTLETT, TN

This is a kid-pleaser, and adults love it too! It's great for parties, tailgating or movie night. Make it festive with red and green candy-coated chocolates. Make a big batch and keep it on hand!

Combine all ingredients except melting chocolate in a large bowl; toss to mix and set aside. Melt chocolate in a double boiler or a microwave; stir until smooth. Slowly pour melted chocolate over cereal mixture; stir to coat evenly. Spread mixture on a wax or parchment paper-lined baking sheet. Cool; break apart and store in an airtight container or large plastic zipping bag.

Makes 16 servings.

- 5 c. bite-size crispy corn or rice cereal squares, or a mixture of both
- 4 c. doughnut-shaped oat cereal
- 2 c. pretzel sticks, coarsely broken
- 2 c. dry-roasted peanuts
- 12-oz. pkg. plain or peanut butter candy-coated chocolates
- 24-oz. pkg. white melting chocolate, broken up

STRUFFOLI

PAM LITTEL
PLEASANT VIEW, TN

Struffoli has been made by our family for generations. Every year, between Christmas and New Year's, my children and I spend a day rolling, cutting and frying. The time we spend cooking and talking is priceless.

2 c. all-purpose flour
1/4 t. salt
3 eggs
1 t. vanilla extract
oil for frying
1 c. honey
1 T. sugar
Optional: sprinkles

In a large bowl, whisk together flour and salt. Add eggs, one at time, mixing well by hand. Stir in vanilla. Turn dough out onto a lightly floured surface and knead, 5 minutes, until smooth. Divide dough in half and roll out each half to form a 1/4-inch thick rectangle. Cut rectangle into 1/4-inch wide strips and roll each strip into a pencil shape, about 7 inches long. Slice each pencil-shaped roll into 1/4 to 1/2-inch pieces. Add enough oil to a deep skillet to equal 2 inches. Over medium-high heat, fry several pieces of dough at a time until golden. Drain on paper towels; place in a large bowl. Repeat with remaining dough. In a small skillet over low heat, cook honey and sugar together for 5 minutes. Remove from heat and drizzle over fried pieces; stir gently to coat. Remove from bowl with a slotted spoon; arrange on a large platter. Decorate with sprinkles, if desired. Refrigerate until ready to serve.

Serves 12.

PRESENTATION

Wrap sandwiches for your garden party in wax paper and tie with a length of gingham ribbon. Serve them in a favorite basket lined with a vintage tea towel.

MINI PECAN TARTLETS

BRITTANY CRAWFORD
FRIENDSHIP, TN

My kids love these yummy little individual pies...they're easy to make too! After the tartlets have cooled, you can dress them up with a spoonful of whipped cream and a pecan half on top.

Blend cream cheese and 1/2 cup butter; mix in flour. Cover and chill while making filling. In a separate bowl, mix together remaining ingredients. Form chilled dough into 24 small balls. Press each ball into the bottom and up the sides of a greased mini muffin cup to form a crust. Spoon in pecan filling. Bake at 350 degrees for 15 to 20 minutes, until golden.

Makes 2 dozen.

1/2 c. cream cheese, softened
1/2 c. plus 1 t. butter, softened and divided
1 c. all-purpose flour
3/4 c. brown sugar, packed
1 egg, beaten
1 t. vanilla extract
1/8 t. salt
1 c. chopped pecans

GRANNY HODGE'S TEA CAKES

JULIE MARSH
SHELBYVILLE, TN

My Granny Hodge gave me a copy of this recipe when I was young and starting my own recipe collection. Years later, after Granny had passed away, my aunt gave me a copy of Granny's same hand-written recipe with a little note, "Mama used to make these for us all when we were kids." I always think of my Mom and Granny Hodge while making these cookies at Christmastime for my family.

Mix together 2 cups sugar and remaining ingredients. Roll out on a floured surface to 1/8-inch thick. Cut with favorite Christmas cookie cutters. Sprinkle lightly with reserved sugar. Transfer to lightly greased baking sheets. Bake at 400 degrees for 10 to 12 minutes, until golden.

Makes 2 dozen.

2-1/4 c. sugar, divided
3 eggs, beaten
5 c. all-purpose flour
2 T. buttermilk
1 c. butter, softened
1 t. baking soda
1 t. vanilla extract

PEANUT BUTTER DROPS

**FAITH HARRIS
ORLINDA, TN**

My mother used to make this fudge for the 10 of us kids when we were growing up. Our family didn't have a lot of money, so it was perfect for us. I think of my mother when I make this fudge. My daughter won first place with this recipe when she entered it in the county fair for her 4-H project.

1/2 c. creamy or crunchy peanut butter
2 c. sugar
1 t. vanilla extract
1 c. milk

Combine peanut butter, milk and sugar in a large heavy saucepan over medium heat. Cook until mixture reaches the soft-ball stage, or 234 to 243 degrees on a candy thermometer. Add vanilla; beat with an electric mixer on low speed until fudge begins to lose its gloss. Immediately drop onto wax paper by tablespoonfuls. Let stand at room temperature until set.

Makes about 1-1/2 dozen.

GRANDPA JIM'S CAKE

**SHEILA GWALTNEY
JOHNSON CITY, TN**

Unbelievably scrumptious!

18-1/4 oz. pkg. German chocolate cake mix
14-oz. can sweetened condensed milk
3/4 c. butterscotch ice cream topping
8-oz. container frozen whipped topping, thawed
2 1.4-oz. chocolate-covered toffee bars, crushed

Prepare cake as directed on package; bake in a 13"x9" baking pan. Poke holes in cake while still warm; pour condensed milk and ice cream topping over cake. Cool. Frost with whipped topping; top with crushed candy. Keep refrigerated.

Makes 12 to 16 servings.

KIPPLENS

SUSAN BOHANNON
SPRING HILL, TN

My Great-Aunt Hilda used to make these cookies during the holidays and my brothers, cousins and I would practically eat them all. They're so delicious! We have passed this recipe down through the generations and now my daughters bake them as well.

In a large bowl, beat butter until fluffy; add remaining ingredients except garnish in order given. Dough will be very stiff. Pinch and roll dough into walnut-size balls. Place on ungreased baking sheets, about one inch apart. Bake at 325 degrees for 28 minutes. While still warm, roll each cookie first in powdered sugar, then in granulated sugar until coated on all sides.

Makes 2 dozen.

2 c. butter, softened
1 c. sugar
1/4 t. salt
5 c. all-purpose flour
2 t. vanilla extract
2 c. chopped pecans
Garnish: powdered
  sugar, additional
  sugar

CAROL'S SOPAIPILLA BARS

CAROL HICKMAN
KINGSPORT, TN

These cream-filled bars are delicious any time of day, even with a cup of tea or coffee at breakfast.

Press one tube crescent rolls into an ungreased 13"x9" baking pan; set aside. Combine cream cheese, one cup sugar and vanilla in a small bowl. Spread cream cheese mixture over crescents in baking pan. Arrange remaining crescent rolls over cream cheese layer. In a small bowl, combine remaining sugar and cinnamon; sprinkle over crescents. Drizzle melted butter over top. Bake at 350 degrees for 25 to 30 minutes. Cool to room temperature; slice into bars.

Makes about 1-1/2 dozen.

2 8-oz. tubes
  refrigerated crescent
  rolls, divided
8-oz. pkg. cream cheese,
  softened
1-1/2 c. sugar, divided
1 t. vanilla extract
1 t. cinnamon
1/2 c. butter, melted

CARAMEL APPLE TARTS

LYNSEY JACKSON
MARYVILLE, TN

My husband is a youth pastor, so we are at the church when the doors open, and our congregation LOVES to eat. I am asked to bring these sweet treats to every gathering. They're always gone before everyone can get through the buffet line, so you'd better make 2 or 3 batches!

3 Braeburn or Fuji apples, cored, peeled and chopped
1-1/2 c. orange juice
3 to 4 T. caramel ice cream topping
1 t. cinnamon
17.3-oz. pkg. frozen puff pastry sheets, thawed
Garnish: additional caramel ice cream topping, cinnamon

Combine apples, orange juice, caramel topping and cinnamon in a medium saucepan over medium heat. Cook until apples are tender; set aside. Cut each pastry sheet into 9 squares. Press squares into lightly greased mini muffin cups; spoon apples into cups. Bake at 350 degrees for 15 to 20 minutes. Garnish with additional caramel topping and cinnamon.

Makes 1-1/2 dozen.

CHESS SQUARES

KAYE SMITH
JACKSON, TN

Always a hit with my family & friends! Very easy to make.

18-1/2 oz. pkg. yellow or butter pecan cake mix
4 eggs, room temperature
1/2 c. margarine, room temperature
1 t. vanilla extract
8-oz. pkg. cream cheese, room temperature
16-oz. pkg. powdered sugar

Beat together cake mix, one egg, margarine and vanilla. Press evenly into the bottom of a lightly greased 13"x9" glass baking pan; set aside. In a separate bowl, beat together cream cheese and remaining eggs. Slowly add powdered sugar; beat until well mixed. Spoon over crust mixture. Bake at 375 degrees for 30 to 40 minutes, until golden and center feels slightly firm. Cool; cut into squares. Store in an airtight container.

Makes 1-1/2 dozen.

RING
L
COOKEVILLE
MARYVILLE
JULIET
OAK RIDGE
MORRISTOWN - BRISTOL

SOUTHERN CARAMEL PIE

JUDY COLLINS
NASHVILLE, TN

Here in Nashville, one of the country clubs always served the most delicious caramel pie made with sweetened condensed milk. This recipe is an easy way to make that wonderful tasting caramel pie in the slow cooker.

Pour condensed milk into a slow cooker that has been sprayed with non-stick vegetable spray. Cover and cook on low setting for 3-1/2 to 4 hours, stirring every 15 minutes after 2-1/2 hours. Cooking time could vary depending on size of your slow cooker. Mixture will appear lumpy, but will thin with stirring. Spoon into crust (the mixture should be golden and should be spooned in before it gets too thick). Chill well. Top with whipped topping and chocolate chips if desired.

Makes 6 to 8 servings.

2 14-oz. cans sweetened
  condensed milk
9-inch graham cracker
  crust
Garnish: whipped
  topping
Optional: mini semi-
  sweet chocolate chips

TENNESSEE MUD CAKE IN A CAN

CHARLOTTE CROCKETT
PALMYRA, TN

Mix up the flavor of this tasty cake by using peanut butter chips or white chocolate chips instead of the semi-sweet ones.

In a bowl, combine dry mixes, sour cream, eggs, water and oil; mix well until smooth. Stir in chocolate chips. Spoon batter into a greased 32-ounce metal coffee can. Set can in a slow cooker. Cover and cook on low setting for 3 to 4 hours, until a toothpick inserted in the center of cake comes out with moist crumbs. Top scoops of cake with a scoop of chocolate ice cream.

Serves 4 to 6.

2 c. chocolate cake mix
1/2 c. instant chocolate
  pudding mix
2 c. sour cream
4 eggs, beaten
1 c. water
3/4 c. oil
1-1/2 c. semi-sweet
  chocolate chips
Garnish: chocolate ice
  cream

POL'S APPLE CAKE

**JEANA OWENS
CUMBERLAND GAP, TN**

I take this cake to church dinners and family reunions...everybody loves it! It is our pastor's favorite cake. I often bake one for him to take home and enjoy. I got this recipe from a telephone bill flyer years ago, and have made this cake often.

3 eggs, beaten
1-1/4 c. oil
2 c. sugar
2-1/2 c. self-rising flour
2 apples, peeled, cored and chopped
1 c. sweetened flaked coconut
1 c. chopped nuts

BROWN SUGAR SAUCE
1/4 c. butter
1/3 c. evaporated milk
1/2 c. brown sugar, packed

In a large bowl, blend eggs, oil and sugar until creamy. Add flour a little at a time, mixing well. Fold in apples, coconut and nuts. Spoon batter into a greased and floured tube pan. Bake at 350 degrees for 30 minutes. Remove from oven; set pan on a wire rack and let cool for a full 30 minutes. Turn cake out of pan onto a serving plate; drizzle warm cake with warm Brown Sugar Sauce.

Brown Sugar Sauce:

Combine all ingredients in a saucepan over medium-low heat. Boil for 3 minutes, stirring until brown sugar dissolves.

Serves 12 to 15.

SUPER FUDGY PIE

ANGELA LIVELY
BAXTER, TN

Top with scoops of vanilla ice cream...yum!

Combine butter, eggs and sugar; mix well. Add cocoa, flour and vanilla; stir until blended. Pour into pie crust. Bake for 30 minutes at 350 degrees. Cool before cutting.

Serves 6 to 8.

1/2 c. butter, melted and cooled
2 eggs, beaten
1 c. sugar
1/4 c. baking cocoa
1/4 c. all-purpose flour
1 t. vanilla extract
9-inch pie crust

HONEY-OATMEAL CAKE

MEGAN BROOKS
ANTIOCH, TN

Simple, yet simply scrumptious! An old family favorite...we used to wrap up slices of this cake to tuck in our picnic basket.

Combine oats, butter and boiling water in a large bowl; stir well and let stand for 20 minutes. Add honey, vanilla and eggs; mix well. In a separate bowl, mix remaining ingredients except frosting. Add flour mixture to oat mixture; stir well. Pour into a greased and floured 13"x9" baking pan. Bake at 350 degrees for 30 to 40 degrees, until a toothpick tests done. Cool; spread with frosting.

Makes 12 servings.

1 c. long-cooking oats, uncooked
1/2 c. butter
1-1/4 c. boiling water
1-1/2 c. honey
1 t. vanilla extract
2 eggs, beaten
1-3/4 c. whole-wheat flour
1 t. baking soda
3/4 t. salt
1 t. cinnamon
1/4 t. nutmeg
Garnish: 16-oz. container coconut-pecan frosting

MEMAW'S PEAR BUNDT CAKE

**BETTY LOU WRIGHT
HENDERSONVILLE, TN**

Decades ago, my mother-in-law used to make this moist, delicious cake during the holiday season. I still treasure her handwritten recipe card. When she died, my aunt took over the job of baking the cake, and now I feel the two of them beside me whenever my kitchen fills with the so-good smells of pears and cinnamon.

2 c. sugar
3 eggs, beaten
1-1/2 c. oil
3 c. all-purpose flour
1 t. baking soda
1 t. salt
1 t. vanilla extract
2 t. cinnamon
3 c. Bartlett pears, peeled, cored and thinly sliced

In a large bowl, combine sugar, eggs and oil; beat well. In a separate bowl, mix flour, baking soda and salt. Add flour mixture to sugar mixture, one cup at a time, mixing well after each addition. Stir in remaining ingredients. Spoon batter into a well greased 10" Bundt® pan. Bake at 350 degrees for one hour, or until a toothpick tests done. Turn cake out of pan onto a plate; cool. Drizzle with Powdered Sugar Glaze.

Powdered Sugar Glaze:
Stir together ingredients, adding milk to a drizzling consistency.

Makes 16 servings.

POWDERED SUGAR GLAZE
1-1/2 c. powdered sugar
2 to 3 T. milk

PEACH & BLUEBERRY COBBLER

AMANDA CLARK
BRISTOL, TN

My friends are always impressed when I serve this dessert...there are never any leftovers! If you want to double the recipe, use a 13"x9" baking pan and bake for 30 to 40 minutes.

Spread peaches in the bottom of an ungreased 8"x8" baking pan. Drain blueberries and spread over peaches; sprinkle with cinnamon. Add quick bread mix to melted butter; stir together. Allow mixture to cool slightly; crumble evenly over blueberries. Sprinkle with cinnamon. Bake at 350 degrees for 20 to 30 minutes, or until golden. Serve warm with ice cream.

Serves 4.

15-oz. can sliced peaches, drained
17.8-oz. pkg. blueberry quick bread mix with canned blueberries
cinnamon to taste
1/2 c. butter, melted
Garnish: vanilla ice cream

HAYSTACKS

BECCA JONES
JACKSON, TN

This recipe is a favorite and so easy to make. A co-worker and friend used to make this treat for the office girls...they look like little haystacks! She was kind enough to share the recipe with us.

In a large saucepan over low heat, melt butterscotch chips. Remove from heat. Add noodles and peanuts; mix well. Drop by tablespoonfuls onto wax paper; allow to set.

Makes 2 dozen.

12-oz. pkg. butterscotch chips
8-oz. can salted cocktail peanuts
5-oz. can chow mein noodles

CUP OF COBBLER

DONNA ELLIOTT
WINCHESTER, TN

My simple fruit cobbler recipe tastes as good as my granny's!

1/2 c. butter, sliced
1 c. all-purpose flour
1 c. sugar
1 c. milk
15-oz. can sliced
   peaches, cherries or
   blackberries in syrup

Add butter to a lightly greased one-quart casserole dish; melt in a 350-degree oven. In a bowl, stir together flour, sugar and milk; pour batter into melted butter. Pour undrained fruit over top; do not stir. Bake at 350 degrees for 30 to 40 minutes, until bubbly and golden. Serve warm.

Serves 4 to 6.

GRANNY RUTH'S APPLE DUMPLINGS

JULIE MARSH
SHELBYVILLE, TN

I'm sharing this recipe in memory of Granny Ruth Wells of Petersburg, Tennessee...she used to make these dumplings for all us kids with lots of love!

2 Granny Smith apples,
   peeled, cored and
   quartered
8-oz. tube refrigerated
   crescent rolls
1/8 t. cinnamon
1 c. sugar, divided
1/2 c. margarine
1/2 c. orange juice
1 t. vanilla extract

Wrap each apple piece in one crescent roll triangle. Arrange in an ungreased 13"x9" baking pan. Sprinkle with cinnamon and one tablespoon sugar. In a saucepan, combine margarine, remaining sugar and orange juice; cook over medium heat until mixture thickens. Remove from heat; stir in vanilla. Pour over dumplings. Bake at 350 degrees for 30 minutes, or until golden. Spoon pan drippings over rolls; serve warm.

Makes 8.

GG'S LADY FINGERS CANDY

CAROL HICKMAN
KINGSPORT, TN

My husband's grandmother GG, as she liked to be called, had always made this delicious candy for Christmas. Whenever visitors stopped by, she pulled out a tin of candy for them to enjoy. For many years she managed to avoid giving me the recipe, but one December my teenage daughter helped her make the candy. At the end of the day, GG sent home a copy of the recipe for me. That was the highlight of my holiday!

In a large bowl, combine all ingredients except butter, chocolate chips and paraffin. Pour melted butter over mixture; stir to combine. Chill one to 2 hours. Form tablespoonfuls of mixture into "fingers" and place on wax paper-lined baking sheets. Chill an additional one to 2 hours. In the top of a double boiler, combine chocolate chips and paraffin over low heat. Stir until completely melted and smooth. With a fork, dip "fingers" into chocolate. Allow excess chocolate to drip back into pan; place on wax paper to cool. Keep refrigerated.

Makes about 5 dozen.

- 16-oz. pkg. powdered sugar
- 1 c. pecans or walnuts, finely chopped
- 2 c. sweetened flaked coconut
- 1 c. graham cracker crumbs
- 1 c. marshmallow creme
- 1 c. creamy peanut butter
- 1 t. vanilla extract
- 1 c. butter, melted
- 12-oz. pkg. semi-sweet chocolate chips
- 1/2 bar paraffin wax, chopped

OLD-FASHIONED BANANA PUDDING

RENEE JOHNSON
COOKEVILLE, TN

My grandmother always made this delicious banana pudding with meringue topping from scratch. It's just right, not too sweet. I like to make it just like she did. I always get rave reviews and often hear, "This is the best banana pudding I've ever had."

3 egg yolks
1 c. sugar
1/4 c. all-purpose flour
1-1/2 c. milk
1/4 c. butter
1 t. vanilla extract
11-oz. pkg. vanilla wafers
4 to 5 ripe bananas, sliced

Combine egg yolks, sugar, flour and milk in the top of a double boiler. Cook and stir over medium heat until thickened to a custard consistency. Remove from heat; blend in butter and vanilla. Place a layer of vanilla wafers and sliced bananas in an ungreased 9"x9" baking pan. Cover with a layer of custard; repeat layers, ending with custard. (Some vanilla wafers may be left over.) Make Meringue; spread over pudding, sealing to edges. Bake at 300 degrees for 15 to 20 minutes, until meringue is golden. Best served warm.

MERINGUE
3 egg whites
1/8 t. cream of tartar
6 T. sugar

Meringue:
In a deep bowl, beat egg whites with an electric mixer on high speed until soft peaks form. Add sugar and cream of tartar; beat until stiff peaks form.

Makes 8 to 10 servings.

APPLE CUPCAKES WITH CARAMEL ICING

TENA HUCKLEBY
MORRISTOWN, TN

This recipe is my own creation. My family especially likes apples and I like caramel. These cupcakes are perfect for fall!

In a large bowl, combine dry cake mix and eggs; mix well. Slowly stir in cider. Fold in remaining ingredients; beat well and set aside. Fill 24 paper-lined muffin cups 2/3 full of batter. Bake at 350 degrees for 20 minutes, or until cupcakes test done with a toothpick. Cool cupcakes on a wire rack. Frost with Caramel Icing. Store in an airtight container.

Caramel Icing:
Grease a large saucepan with one tablespoon butter. Add remaining butter, sugar, milk and corn syrup. Mix well over medium-high heat. Bring to a boil; boil until mixture reaches the soft-ball stage, or 234 to 243 degrees on a candy thermometer. Remove from heat; stir in vanilla. Cool slightly. Beat with an electric mixer on medium speed until creamy.

Makes 2 dozen.

15-1/4 oz. pkg. golden butter cake mix
2 eggs, beaten
1 c. apple cider
1/2 t. cinnamon
1/4 c. light brown sugar, packed
1 c. apples, peeled, cored and chopped

CARAMEL ICING
5 T. butter, softened and divided
1-1/2 c. light corn syrup
3 c. sugar
1 t. vanilla extract
2 c. milk

INDEX

INDEX continued

U.S. to METRIC RECIPE EQUIVALENTS

Volume Measurements

¼ teaspoon. . . . . 1 mL
½ teaspoon. . . . . 2 mL
1 teaspoon . . . . 5 mL
1 tablespoon = 3 teaspoons. . . . . . 15 mL
2 tablespoons = 1 fluid ounce . . . . 30 mL
¼ cup. . . . . 60 mL
⅓ cup. . . . . 75 mL
½ cup = 4 fluid ounces. . . . . 125 mL
1 cup = 8 fluid ounces . . . . 250 mL
2 cups = 1 pint = 16 fluid ounces 500 mL
4 cups = 1 quart . . . . 1 L

Weights

1 ounce . . . . 30 g
4 ounces . . . . 120 g
8 ounces . . . . 225 g
16 ounces = 1 pound . . . . 450 g

Baking Pan Sizes

Square
8x8x2 inches . . . . 2 L = 20x20x5 cm
9x9x2 inches . . . . . . 2.5 L = 23x23x5 cm

Rectangular
13x9x2 inches . . . . . 3.5 L = 33x23x5 cm

Loaf
9x5x3 inches . . . . 2 L = 23x13x7 cm

Round
8x1½ inches . . . . 1.2 L = 20x4 cm
9x1½ inches . . . . 1.5 L = 23x4 cm

Recipe Abbreviations

t. = teaspoon. . . . . ltr. = liter
T. = tablespoon. . . . . oz. = ounce
c. = cup. . . . . lb. = pound
pt. = pint. . . . . .doz. = dozen
qt. = quart. . . . . .pkg. = package
gal. = gallon. . . . . .env. = envelope

Oven Temperatures

300° F. . . . . .150° C
325° F. . . . . .160° C
350° F. . . . . .180° C
375° F. . . . . .190° C
400° F. . . . . .200° C
450° F. . . . . .230° C

Kitchen Measurements

A pinch = ⅛ tablespoon
1 fluid ounce = 2 tablespoons
3 teaspoons = 1 tablespoon
4 fluid ounces = ½ cup
2 tablespoons = ⅛ cup
8 fluid ounces = 1 cup
4 tablespoons = ¼ cup
16 fluid ounces = 1 pint
8 tablespoons = ½ cup
32 fluid ounces = 1 quart
16 tablespoons = 1 cup
16 ounces net weight = 1 pound
2 cups = 1 pint
4 cups = 1 quart
4 quarts = 1 gallon

Send us your favorite recipe

and the memory that makes it special for you!*

If we select your recipe for a brand-new **Gooseberry Patch** cookbook, your name will appear right along with it...and you'll receive a FREE copy of the book!

Submit your recipe on our website at

www.gooseberrypatch.com/sharearecipe

*Please include the number of servings and all other necessary information.

Have a taste for more?

Visit www.gooseberrypatch.com to join our Circle of Friends!

• Free recipes, tips and ideas plus a complete cookbook index
• Get mouthwatering recipes and special email offers delivered to your inbox.

You'll also love these cookbooks from **Gooseberry Patch**!

A Year of Holidays
The Best Instant Pot® Cookbook
Fresh Farmhouse Recipes
From Grandma's Recipe Box
Grandma's Best Comfort Foods
Mom's Go-To Recipes
Our Best Farm-Fresh Recipes
Our Best Quick & Easy Casseroles
Quick & Easy Recipes for Gatherings
Smart & Easy Meal Planning

www.gooseberrypatch.com